129406

Open Guides to Literature

Series Editor: Graham Martin (Professor of Literature, The Open University)

Titles in the Series

Angus Calder: Byron
Jenni Calder: *Animal Farm* and *1984*
Walford Davies: Dylan Thomas
Roger Day: Larkin
Peter Faulkner: Yeats
P. N. Furbank: Pound
Brean Hammond: *Gulliver's Travels*
Graham Holderness: *Hamlet*
Graham Holderness: *Women in Love*
Graham Holderness: *Wuthering Heights*
Jeannette King: *Jane Eyre*
Graham Martin: *Great Expectations*
David B. Pirie: Shelley
Jeremy Tambling: What is Literary Language?
Dennis Walder: Ted Hughes
Roderick Watson: MacDiarmid

JEREMY TAMBLING

What Is Literary Language?

Open University Press
Milton Keynes · Philadelphia

129406

Open University Press
Open University Educational Enterprises Limited
12 Cofferidge Close
Stony Stratford
Milton Keynes MK11 1BY, England
and
242 Cherry Street
Philadelphia, PA 19106, USA

First Published 1988

British Library Cataloguing in Publication Data

Tambling, Jeremy
   What is literary language? – (Open guides
   to literature).
   1. Literature. Language
   I. Title
   808

   ISBN 0-335-09016-8
   ISBN 0-335-09015-X Pbk

Library of Congress Cataloging in Publication Data

Tambling, Jeremy.
   What is literary language? – Jeremy Tambling.
      p. cm. – (Open guides to literature)
   Bibliography: p.
   Includes index.
   1. Style, Literary.   2. English language – Style.   3. Language and
   languages.   I. Title.   II. Series.
   PN203.T35 1988   808 – dc19   88-1812   CIP
   ISBN 0-335-09016-8
   ISBN 0-335-09015-X (pbk)

Typeset by Rowland Phototypesetting Limited
Bury St Edmunds, Suffolk
Printed in Great Britain by
J. W. Arrowsmith Limited, Bristol

Contents

Series Editor's Preface   vii

Acknowledgements   ix

1   Literary Language and Literature: An Introduction   1

2   British and American Concepts of Literature   10

3   Modernism and Formalism   22

4   Language Structures in Literature   36

5   Language, Rhetoric, Meaning   54

6   Meaning and Literary Language   69

7   Some Conclusions   84

Appendix: Critical, Rhetorical and Technical Terms   98

Notes   107

Further Reading   113

Index of Names   115

Series Editor's Preface

The intention of this series is to provide short introductory books about major writers, texts, and literary concepts for students of courses in Higher Education which substantially or wholly involve the study of Literature.

The series adopts a pedagogic approach and style similar to that of Open University material for Literature courses. *Open Guides* aim to inculcate the reading 'skills' which many introductory books in the field tend, mistakenly, to assume that the reader already possesses. They are, in this sense, 'teacherly' texts, planned and written in a manner which will develop in the reader the confidence to undertake further independent study of the topic. They are 'open' in two senses. First, they offer a three-way tutorial exchange between the writer of the *Guide*, the text or texts in question, and the reader. They invite readers to join in an exploratory discussion of texts, concentrating on their key aspects and on the main problems which readers, coming to the texts for the first time, are likely to encounter. The flow of a *Guide* 'discourse' is established by putting questions for the reader to follow up in a tentative and searching spirit, guided by the writer's comments, but not dominated by an over-arching and single-mindedly-pursued argument or evaluation, which itself requires to be 'read'.

Guides are also 'open' in a second sense. They assume that literary texts are 'plural', that there is no end to interpretation, and that it is for the reader to undertake the pleasurable task of discovering meaning and value in such texts. *Guides* seek to provide, in compact form, such relevant biographical, historical and cultural information as bears upon the reading of the text, and they point the reader to a selection of the best available critical discussions of it. They are not in themselves concerned to propose, or to counter, particular readings of the texts, but rather to put *Guide* readers in a position to do that for themselves. Experienced travellers learn to dispense with guides, and so it should be for readers of this series.

Graham Martin

Acknowledgements

Handling theoretical material in the short space available in this book inevitably means simplifying, and not allowing oppositional voices to be heard quite enough. The endnotes, and the suggestions for further reading are intended to raise the possibility of a debate centring on the issues in the text.

Many of the examples in this book have been tried out on students, particularly those in the past eight years, (1980–1987), at Open University literature Summer Schools at York. They, and friends teaching with me on those courses, have contributed extensively, and sometimes unawares, to my ideas on the topic here. I am grateful to all, but will not mention names apart from Stewart Hamblin, always beforehand in reading and thinking. For pushing me towards Jakobson's work, I would like to thank another now very ex-student of mine, Ian Fairley.

For detailed and helpful criticism of the drafts of this book, I am grateful to Graham Martin, the general editor of the series. For comments on the Shakespeare material I thank John Coldewey. For suggestions and for discussions over the issues here, conducted over several years, I would thank Bob Pattison. Chris Barlow gave useful comments on the last draft of the book, as did Ray Cunningham, of the Open University Press.

And Pauline I would thank for her stoical acceptance of the idea of another book being written in the house. Again, I would dedicate this book to her.

The author and publisher wish to thank the following for their permission to reproduce copyright material:

Faber and Faber and Alfred A. Knopf Inc. for an extract from *The collected works of Wallace Stevens*; The Society of Authors, Jonathan Cape and Viking Press and Penguin Inc. for extracts from James Joyce: *A portrait of the artist as a young man* and *Finnegans*

Wake; Bob Dylan for an extract from *Writings and Drawings*; the estate of Virginia Woolf, the Hogarth Press and Harcourt Brace Jovanovich, Inc. for an extract from Virginia Woolf: *Mrs Dalloway* and Century Hutchinson for an extract from *A Scot's Quair*; Grassic Gibbon: 'Let it go' from *Collected Poems of William Empson*, copyright 1949, 1977 by William Empson is reprinted by permission of Harcourt Brace Jovanovich, Inc. and the estate of the author and The Hogarth Press.

Is not *literary* language the name we give to a diction whose frame of reference is such that words stand out as words (even as sounds) rather than being, at once assimilable meanings? The meaning of words is not unimportant, of course; it is deviation from normal use that suggests that something is wrong with speaker or hearer, with the source or the receiver. For instance, two persons (voices) may be trying to get through at the same time; or perhaps we have come in at the wrong point, and cannot follow. To call a text literary is to *trust* that it will make sense eventually, even though its quality of reference may be complex, disturbed, unclear. It is a way of 'saving the phenomena' of words that are out of the ordinary or bordering the nonsensical – that have no stabilised reference.

Geoffrey Hartman: *Saving the Text*

We do not know where metaphor begins and ends. An abstract word is formed through the sublimation of a concrete word. A concrete word, which never designates the object except through one of its qualities, is itself only a metaphor or at the very least a figurative expression. Moreover, the designation of an object using an expression that would correspond to it – not a figurative expression, but a literal one – would require the knowledge of the very essence of this object, which is impossible, since we can only know phenomena, and not things in themselves.

Not only language, but all intellectual life rests on a play of transpositions and symbols that one can characterise as metaphorical. Furthermore, knowledge always proceeds through comparison, so that all known objects are linked through relations of interdependence. It is not possible to determine, between two given entities, which is designated by the name proper to it, the name that is not the metaphor of the other, and vice versa. Man is a mobile tree, just as the tree is a deep-rooted man. In the same way, the sky is a rarefied earth, the earth a thickened sky. And if I see a dog run, it's just as much the run that dogs.

Michel Leiris: 'Metaphore', *Brisées*

1. Literary Language and Literature: An Introduction

What then is this language that says nothing, is never silent, and is called 'literature'?

　　　　　Michel Foucault: *The Order of Things*

In Molière's comedy, *Le Bourgeois Gentilhomme*, (1670), the primary target is the philistinism of the middle-class and middle-aged merchant, M. Jourdain, who wants to buy aristocratic Culture with money. Jourdain hires a philosophy master to tell him all the things about language that he does not know, and is very impressed when he learns that he can only write a love-letter in verse or prose, because those are the only things there are, and that he must therefore have been speaking prose all his life without knowing it. Molière's standpoint is, of course, one of sturdy commonsense, from which he ridicules pretentiousness brilliantly. But without getting too much like M. Jourdain, it is still possible to wonder if there is something more to writing than that sturdy division of things into one medium or the other.

　　Deciding how to tell the two things apart often ends in difficulties. The influential English critic F. R. Leavis (1895–1978) described novels such as those by Dickens, George Eliot and Lawrence as 'dramatic poems'. The Russian critic Mikhail Bakhtin, (1895–1975) in his posthumously published work on the novel called *The Dialogic Imagination*, found novels, which most people think of as being written in prose and dating, on the whole, from around the post-Renaissance world, in places where other critics /people saw classical epics or romances, and virtually stopped discussing the genre at the moment when people might have thought he was ready to get into the subject – in the post-Renaissance.

Wordsworth, in the Preface to the *Lyrical Ballads*, (1798) found no difference between prose and poetry. Matthew Arnold magisterially described the two eighteenth-century poets Dryden and Pope as 'classics of our prose'. So perhaps there is a question still to be faced: there is both prose and poetry but we are not quite sure which is which.

We could be sceptical of that doubt, and point out that the people so far quoted are using categories and then deliberately breaking them up – novel, poetry, epic, romance, and so on – simply to make a rhetorical point. They could not have used the terms at all if there was not a general sense of what they are meaning. An argument that the novel was really a poem could only make sense if people were thereby stirred up to rethink conventional divisions, whereby we knew what prose was and what poetry consisted in.

There is obviously truth in that argument, but it makes us ask a question one further back. If it is important that writing and criticism should make people feel that they did not know their way about, that they have been made to see things differently, ('make it new' was the demand of Ezra Pound for poetry) how did we get to know what was standard poetry, or standard prose? How did we get to a stage where we thought we knew what was literature and what was not? Is it because educational practices have taught people to make clear distinctions between different types of writing?

Read the following pieces. Now think how you would characterize them. Are they verse or prose? Literature or not literature? Literary or non-literary? What features are distinctive about each? Though it is a separate exercise, you may also find it useful to try to assign a rough date to the passages.

1   In such condition, there is no place for Industry; because the fruit thereof is uncertain: and consequently no Culture of the Earth, no Navigation, nor use of the commodities that may be imported by Sea; no commodious building; no instruments of moving and removing such things as require much force; no Knowledge of the face of the Earth; no account of Time; no Arts; no Letters, no Society; and which is worst of all, continuall feare and danger of violent death; And the life of man, solitary, poor, nasty, brutish, and short.

2   Let those who feast at Ease on dainty fare
Pity the Reapers, who their Feasts prepare:
For Toils scarce ever ceasing press us now;
Rest never does, but on the Sabbath, show;
And barely that our Masters will allow.
Think what a painful life we daily lead;
Each Morning early rise, go late to Bed;
Nor, when asleep, are we secure from Pain;
We then perform our Labours o'er again . . .

3 The Communists disdain to conceal their views and aims. They openly declare that their ends can be attained only by the forcible overthrow of all existing social conditions. Let the ruling classes tremble at a Communistic revolution. The proletarians have nothing to lose but their chains. They have a world to win.
WORKING MEN OF ALL COUNTRIES, UNITE!

4 Was she beautiful or not beautiful? and what was the secret of form or expression which gave the dynamic quality to her glances? Was the good or the evil genius dominant in those beams? Probably the evil: else why was the effect that of unrest rather than of undisturbed charm? Why was the wish to look again felt as coercion and not as a longing in which the whole being consents?

DISCUSSION

You will probably have decided that only 2 is poetry, and you may possibly decide that 4 is part of a novel, which may have inclined you to put it, like 2, into the category of literature. Perhaps 1, 2, and 4 struck you as using literary effects in the language whereas 3 came across as simpler and more direct altogether. But none of them, probably, seemed very standard English. Taking the pieces in turn, my own comments would go:

1 Prose, clearly, and obviously aimed at persuasion: look at the developing climax, with the frequent repetition of the word 'no . . .', leading up to 'which is worst of all'. Look too at the balancing of ideas. Industry is paired with 'no Culture of the Earth', (i.e. no agriculture): – does the phrase sound vaguely Biblical to you? The ending has a cadence that is clearly derivative from preaching styles, and the whole thing is structured as it is to convey a positive sense of what is lost through anarchy. The passage is from Hobbes' *Leviathan*, part I, ch. XIII, (1651) and is part of a treatise arguing for strong government.

2 As verse, this is set out clearly in a form called the 'heroic couplet', often applied to iambic pentameter verse, where pairs of lines rhyme. In iambic pentameter a line has 10 or 11 syllables and five heavy stresses. It is very familiar in English verse from the Renaissance onwards. But how regular is this? The couplet structure is broken in lines 3–5; is there a reason for this? Would you agree with the argument that the writer has lengthened the couplet here to enforce the idea of the toils never ceasing? (Pope, who wrote like this, did the same thing often.) If that is the case, again the element of persuasion – of rhetoric – enters in. That persuasion comes in strongly at the line 'Think what a painful life . . .'. There is a strong internal structure here. Note the repeated 'ea' that links 'feast . . . ease . . . reaper . . . feasts . . . ceasing', and the internal rhyme –

assonance – that connects 'ceasing' to 'press' and 'rest'. Note the
balancing of ideas in 'early rise, go late': early and late come at the
outside of the phrase in a figure of speech called a chiasmus, as the
two middle verbs also balance each other. Though the passage is
technically well crafted, in the eighteenth-century style, it is also
fairly straightforward; there are signs here of lack of sophistication:
look at the repeated 'painful . . . Pain'. The author is Stephen Duck,
(1705–56), a self-taught poet from Wiltshire, who writes here about
the labourer's existence from personal experience.*

3   This is clearly rhetorical, and persuasive. It ends the *Communist
Manifesto* by Marx and Engels, and though written in 1848, it first
appeared in English translation in 1888. My guess is that you may
have found this the least literary piece. It starts with a direct
statement; indeed, 'The Communists disdain to conceal their views
and aims', which seems to rule out any suggestion of 'literariness' in
the language, makes it 'straight from the shoulder'. But look at its
actual effects: those repeated openings of 'openly . . . only . . .
overthrow . . . all' are an example of an alliteration that helps the
onward flow of language. Note the balancing of a long sentence –
'The proletarians . . .' with a short: 'They have a world to win' – and
see the alliteration there. Though this is not poetry, note, too, the use
of another line and a different emphasis to give force to the last
punch-line. That line is often quoted: the metaphorical reference to
'chains', a fine exaggeration – hyberbole, in rhetorical terms – has
made this more famous than many passages of 'literature'. Is
it because the implicit comparison between the proletariat and
prisoners is so deliberately audacious? (Does the mind, perhaps, in
reading the one word, start thinking of the other, subconsciously,
because they do start with the same letters?)

4   This is the most literary of the pieces: the opening to George
Eliot's novel, *Daniel Deronda* (1876). It is prose, of course, but it
owes a distant debt to Shakespearian blank verse, since its rhythm is
not far from the iambic pentameter. Look at the following lines,
where I have marked the stressed syllables '/' and the unstressed '˘'

        ˘ ˘ / ˘/ ˘ /   / ˘/
    Was she beautiful, or not beautiful?
          ˘ /   ˘ // ˘ / ˘ ˘ ˘ /
    . . . which gave the dynamic quality to her glances?
        ˘ /˘ ˘ / ˘   /   /˘   ˘/
    . . . a longing in which the whole being consents

* The technical terms raised in this paragraph and elsewhere in the book are
discussed in further detail in the Appendix.

When George Eliot refers to 'the good or the evil genius', she is thinking allegorically, about people's qualities as people themselves, in the manner of Shakespearian and earlier drama. In itself, this makes the language 'literary' in an important sense in that it is quoting and remembering earlier literary works. This woman is being thought of hardly as a woman at all, but rather as a symbol: look at the way 'her glance' in one sentence becomes 'those beams' in the next. Note the balancing of 'unrest' with 'undisturbed charm'; and of 'coercion' with 'longing': and see how the word 'coercion' is picked up by alliteration with the word 'consents'. (And there is the . . . on . . . assonance with 'longing' and 'consents'.) This writing is meant to pull the reader on, to lure him/her into reading on, to find out who the fascinating and dangerous woman is. Though I gave both male and female pronouns, I need hardly have bothered with the female, for the person looking, we learn in the next paragraph, is a man, and the idea that is raised in the passage quoted has to do with the perception of women that men are supposed to have: to see them as dangerous, tempting. It is the more ironic, therefore, that it should be a woman who writes thus, and under a male pen-name.

Are these passages, any or some of them, *literature*? All of them use poetic means and a whole armoury of rhetorical devices to persuade the reader – in 1, to accept Hobbes' views of society, in 2 to see the worker as oppressed, in 3 to rise up against the bosses, and to warn them, and in 4, just to read on. All rely on balancing the expected with the surprising: Hobbes finishes with as much of a flourish as Marx, and George Eliot relies on arousing feelings of what the Dangerous Woman is like by asking questions that are going to be answered eventually. Duck uses Pope's methods of making the rhyming couplet work for him, and in that sense, the sense plays against and with the structure of the verse, as with the three lines that rhyme at one point.

   Nothing within their techniques disallows them from the category of literary writing, and the distinctions of prose and poetry make little difference really, since the poetic is contained in the prose, and nothing could be more like simple prose than the Duck. One answer to the question of whether they are literature would be to say that it depends on what you call literature, or rather, who's studying it. When I read English at University, we spent a week on Hobbes, and another on George Eliot. I had not heard of Duck and Marx was not on the reading list. This suggests that literature is a comparatively arbitrarily chosen subject: and what gets put onto the syllabus has strong ideological associations. Nothing very surprising in that. But the consequence that follows from this is – and it goes straight into the subject of this book – if we define 'literary language' as the language that is used in literature, then there are problems: for what is literature?

A couple of examples will help. When Ian Fleming started the James Bond novels, Jonathan Cape, his publishers, envisaged an up-market readership, and packaged them accordingly. Fleming himself wrote in an interview for *Books and Bookmen* (May 1963) that 'while thrillers may not be literature with a capital L, it is possible to write what I can best describe as "thrillers designed to be read as literature"'. The formulation is worth comparing with another example. In the 1930s, Ernest Sutherland Bates produced a volume called *The Bible Designed to be Read as Literature*, with an introduction by Laurence Binyon. What would Christian or Jewish believers think of their sacred book being called 'Literature'? Does this not trivialize the Book, making it seem as though it need only be read for its beauty of expression? But then what would Hobbes have thought of being studied in an English literature seminar? But if you're going to do Hobbes, then why not Marx? And could we imagine a literature department where people studied Duck and not Pope? If not, is that because of the content of either, or because one is famous, the other not?

Consider the implications behind Ian Fleming's and Bates's formulation 'to be read as Literature'. Why cannot thrillers be Literature?

DISCUSSION

'Literature' seems to mean something like 'fine writing', or 'writing with style', and something which clearly has not much to do with content. And it would appear that a text is turned into Literature by the way prestigious publishers, such as Penguin, market it as 'a classic': jacket designs and even pictures of actors with a certain kudos turn texts into Literature. Think how many novel titles are presented with the words 'NOW A MAJOR FILM FROM . . .' on them. This immediately elevates them, sometimes even turns them into Literature. Why thrillers cannot be Literature is not obvious, except that the Literature category seems, in popular thinking, to be the repository of values that are uplifting, while thrillers just entertain.

Non-believers might reply to the title *The Bible Designed to be Read as Literature* by saying that it was just the right title: the Bible *is* literature, because the Bible is fiction. And many might accept the definition that literature = imaginative, and therefore non-factual, so 'untrue' writing. On that basis, clearly George Eliot is writing literature; but what of Duck? As poetry, it seems that it must enter the category of literature. But it also seems to be giving the truth about a situation. But the issue remains teasing. Imagine *The Communist Manifesto Designed to be Read as Literature*. In what way does the decision to call something 'literature' affect the way it is read? Presumably when a text is designated literature, it is read differently. But that only comes back to the issue of how a work comes to be elevated to the status of literature – or marginalized, perhaps, in the case of the Bible – if you believe that it can and should be read for something more than its language.

It was in the nineteenth century that literature gained a specialized meaning.[1] The Latin *littera* means letter, and *litteratura* translates the Greek word *grammatike*, the knowledge of reading and writing. In the seventeenth and eighteenth centuries, the word meant writing, usually writing with some distinction, such as *belles lettres*, a seventeenth century term for writing regarded when it is written now with some disdain (as in the adjective of contempt, 'belletristic') – writing that is self-consciously stylish and that elevates its fine form over its meaning. In the 1860s and 1870s, in Britain, 'literature' began to acquire more specialized associations, and to become not good writing on any topic, but writing in the form of classical or modern poetry ('the crown of literature' according to Matthew Arnold) or drama, or the novel, (though this was always regarded as the poor relation, as far as literature was concerned). Essay writing, memoirs, autobiographies and biographies stood in the shadows: to be regarded as literature or not according to taste. Literature now had a restricted sense: it was writing that appealed to the emotions, and that worked by its distinctive form. Indeed, this new distinction gives the writer a whole further register to use: Marx, for instance, in the gravely witty *The Eighteenth Brumaire of Louis Bonaparte* (1851) uses very self-conscious literary language and terms in order to indicate that nineteenth-century middle-class revolutions are parodies, theatrical displays only, aesthetic exercises, not genuine, not political: hence his beginning: 'Hegel remarks somewhere that all the great events and characters of world history occur, so to speak, twice. He forgot to add, the first time as tragedy, the second as farce'. With this epigrammatic opening in mind, dictating the style of what is to come, Marx writes in a deliberately heightened, baroque, excessive way, to point up the 'farce' – a literary term indeed – that is the coming to power of Napoleon III.

But that new meaning of the word 'literature' also brought with it issues of inclusion and exclusion such as I have described above: the teasing question of what a University department of English

Literature should teach. Much twentieth-century theory, especially that associated with Roman Jakobson, (1896–1982) has tried to define instead a concept of 'literariness', or 'literary language', as the indispensable quality of literature. This is where the argument of this book begins. For in looking at examples 1 to 4, it is apparent that they all use literary language: just as politicians do in speeches, as advertising does, as educationists do, as anyone does when they try to write persuasively to anyone, even a Bank Manager, so that 'literariness' is not at all limited to 'literature'. Thus to the question, 'What is literary language?', the short answer might be, 'There isn't one – if by that you mean some essential quality that marks out a piece of writing as literature'.

I shall be arguing that proposition here, and using it to show that the category of 'literature' cannot be held to have any essential meaning: there is no body of writing that 'ought' to be studied as such, as the repository of 'cultural values' or of important traditions. Yet the argument is not easy, for historically, both the idea of 'literature' and of 'literary language' have meant much; and during the course of the book I shall be quoting definitions of both to show that writers and critics have argued for the categories – which doesn't prove that they exist in any ahistorical, essential manner but indicates that they are necessary terms, and can be used to generate new significances, new meanings.

Many critics would reply fairly impatiently to the objection that literature cannot be defined, saying that these examples were unrepresentative: next to the number of poets, dramatists and novelists who were studied in universities, schools or colleges, Hobbes is obviously someone who could be argued about either way, but is in any case something of a special case, while Marx is clearly much more a matter for a history or politics department. (Though this would pose problems for an adequate reading of *The Eighteenth Brumaire*.) There is a mainstream, clearly, of literature, and there will always be people just in the sidestream. Literary language can, then, be discussed usefully in terms of these figures who are central: the fact that other language users have drawn on literary devices is neither here nor there. Further, the form of a work is indicative of its literary status: poetry, drama, fiction. And the oldest types of writing we have are literary – Homer for instance; just as it seems apparent that poetry is an older form of writing than prose: something certainly borne out in the history of English literature. So that we start with the literary.

What do you think of the argument that we do know what literature is, and that we can work from there?

DISCUSSION

My answer would be that it raises the question of how the main-stream was constituted as such. George Eliot is certainly in it; but that passage from *Daniel Deronda* is an effective reminder that the boundary between 'literature' and 'popular art' – which often enough exploits the idea of the dangerously guileful woman – is very thin, and that if George Eliot is set up as literature, this should encourage us to inspect the ideology implicit in her text. To say 'we know what literature is', and then to mention some famous names – Shakespeare, Milton, Wordsworth – means that we work in a circle: we know what literature is because we have these writers, and the writers set up an imaginary standard where literature is defined in relationship to them. But how did we ever start on this circle?

Further, the argument is in danger of suggesting that what a politics, or history, or philosophy department reads for primary sources does not need looking at on the level of language. Post-structuralist thought, (Jacques Derrida, particularly – see Chapter 6) argues that there is no other level: that you cannot argue about the ideas within a text, you can only analyse its language and the metaphysical views that language subtends. Thus not only the Bible, but also the *Communist Manifesto* and the *Eighteenth Brumaire* and Hobbes *Leviathan* are all literature – that is, writing: and no distinctions of approach can be made about them without short-circuiting the point that these texts exist simply and straight-forwardly, as rhetorical performances: as writing.

If we cannot define our terms easily in some absolute sense, it may be more useful to think about how the terms 'literature' and the concept of 'literary' came into being, and probe their uses. This is what I do in the following chapters. At the end, in the appendix, I have discussed and explained some terms that most people who think about the subject at all might wish to use in discussing 'literary language': you should find definitions of technical terms used in the text there, and further discussion of the rhetorical devices that do indeed structure writing.

2. British and American Concepts of Literature

> I think Poetry should surprise by a fine excess and not by Singularity –
> it should strike the Reader as a wording of his own highest thoughts
> and appear almost a Remembrance . . . its touches of Beauty should
> never be half way there by making the reader breathless instead of
> content: the rise, the progress, the setting of imagery should like the
> Sun come naturally to him – shine over him and set soberly although
> in magnificence leaving him in the Luxury of twilight . . . if Poetry
> comes not as naturally as the Leaves to a tree it had better not come at
> all.
>
> John Keats: *Letters, 27 February 1818*

In this chapter I want to examine some of the significant views about
literature and the 'literary' that have been available in Britain and the
United States: views marked out by a strong empirical bias, and a
refusal to indulge in 'theory'. The Coleridge to Leavis line of English
criticism, and the American New Critics have dealt with the 'creative' or the 'poetic' uses of language, but we shall have to wait for the
next chapter, and specifically for the theorizing of Modernism within
Europe, to find attention being paid to 'literary language'.

Historically, the study of literature in Britain owed much to the
nineteenth century and to the stress of Matthew Arnold (1822–88)
on the 'Function of criticism at the present time', (1867), the title of
an essay written at the time of the Reform Bill, which was designed to
give the vote to the skilled urban worker: actually, it meant that eight
per cent of the population would be able to vote, a situation which
Arnold thought of as anarchy! At this time of political instability,

Arnold recommended culture, as 'the best that is thought and known in the world', to become the basis of national education, to bring people into line, effectively, with the ideas of the ruling classes. An Education Bill was passed in 1870, and the aims of this prescription for education went along with Arnold's ideas for the newly enfranchized; and he picked up on certain aspects of the earlier Coleridge's criticism, as well as on the eighteenth century, to suggest that poetry could be examined closely to prove its greatness. Arnold's essay, 'The study of poetry', (1880) is crucial for his contention that 'poetry is a criticism of life', and that 'the best poetry is what we want: the best poetry will be found to have a power of forming, sustaining, and delighting us, as nothing else can'.[1]

Out of this encouragement that schools and educational establishments should study poetry and literature underlay the development in our century of 'practical criticism' – Coleridge's term. Coleridge defined prose as 'words in their best order' and poetry as 'the *best* words in the best order' (*Table-talk*, 1827, published 1836), and it will do as his sense of what characterizes literary language. Such a view determines what practical criticism is – the minute examination of the words on the page in a poem, in an extract from a play or a novel. Practical criticism has been regarded as the distinctive aspect of the study of English literature: generations now of students at A level and in colleges and universities will have had to compare poems by unseen poets, and make an assessment of their relative worths.

The important point is how new all this was. Up to the time of the Romantic movement, that is, up to roughly 1800, few writers would have thought that they were writing *literature*: they would merely have thought they were engaged in some enterprise – political, rhetorical, dramatic or persuasive – that might have involved style, but certainly was not to be thought of in classic terms. When the word 'literary' appeared in the mid-seventeenth century, its meaning included 'pertaining to the letters of the alphabet', or, later, simply to do with any form of writing. Doctor Johnson in the 1770s belonged to a 'Literary Club', but it had nothing to do with the idea of *literature*: it simply designated those who were interested in writing. That is not to say that the eighteenth century did not think carefully about ways of writing: Dryden (1631–1700) thought in terms of using rules for writing poetry derived from the ancients, and found it 'almost a miracle' that Shakespeare, 'untaught by any . . . should by the force of his own genius perform so much' ('Preface to *All for Love*' (1678)). Alexander Pope (1688–1744) wrote on 'wit' in poetry as being its distinctive quality – meaning by that term something like invention and imagination:

True wit is nature to advantage dressed
What oft was thought, but n'er so well expressed.
                                    (*Essay on criticism*, 1711)

All that fine writing – style – does, then, is to put a fine coating, like
the almond on a wedding cake, on previously thought out ideas.
Pope's heroic couplet works like Duck's, and you will notice how
there is a close fit between the epigrammatic, 'witty' style, and the
closed form of the couplet, which aims at conciseness.

The Romantics thought differently from Pope. Wordsworth,
(1770–1850), defined a poet as 'a man speaking to men' (no special
'wit' then) and, with his stress on emotion rather than on rule-bound
rationality in poetry, defined it as 'the spontaneous overflow of
powerful feelings' in the *Preface to the Lyrical Ballads* (1800).
Literature was becoming something to be theorized. He, and
Coleridge, and Blake, began to think in terms that actively criticized
earlier ways of writing and they suggested that literature had to do
with moral instruction. 'The only end of writing is to enable the
readers better to enjoy life, or better to endure it' Dr Johnson wrote,
in his review of *A Free inquiry into the nature and origin of evil*,
(1757) thus in some ways anticipating this new moral concern, this
sense the Romantics had that poetry was concerned with the question 'how to live?' Shelley defined poetry as 'the expression of the
Imagination',[2] thus giving it an almost religious significance; and
Romantic ideology stressed the poem as marked out by organic
unity. Thus for Coleridge: 'a poem is that species of composition
which is opposed to works of science by proposing for its *immediate*
object pleasure, not truth . . . it is discriminated by proposing to itself
such delight from the *whole* as is compatible with a distinct gratifica-
tion from each component *part*'. (*Biographia Literaria* (1817), ch.
14). As an active organism, a poem builds up to a whole, and each
part can be studied: 'nothing can permanently please, or please long,
which does not contain in itself the reason why it is so and not
otherwise' (*Ibid.*). In his Preface, (1907), to *The Tragic Muse*, Henry
James (1843–1916), the novelist, declared his preference in literature: 'I delight in a deep breathing economy and an organic form'. A
literary work should thus (a) have unity within it, (b) be full of 'life'
and feeling, those Romantic concepts, and (c) be disciplined, relevant, and not given to playfulness.

Wordsworth, Coleridge, Arnold, James – these figures were
instrumental in building up a dominant sense that literature should
be actively criticized, not just read, and accepted or dismissed,
according to the point of view of the reader. To criticize means that
to take account of the moral outlook of the original writer is crucial.

The tradition does not represent every view; it takes no account, for instance of Walter Pater (1839–94), who viewed with alarm the idea of literature teaching moral truths, and felt that its inherent form and beauty was all that mattered; but despite this alternative tradition of aesthetic criticism – 'all art aspires to the condition of music' (Pater); 'all art is quite useless' (Wilde),[3] the dominant trend has been in favour of moral seriousness. 'We must grant the artist his subject, his idea, his *donée*: our criticism is applied only to what he makes of it' said Henry James, in his essay 'The art of fiction'. In his Preface (1907) to *A Portrait of a Lady*, he spoke of the 'dependence of the "moral" sense of the work on the amount of felt life concerned in producing it'. In the twentieth century, this moral sense of literature and criticism was maintained by such figures as D. H. Lawrence, T. S. Eliot, I. A. Richards, William Empson, his pupil, and, most famously, by F. R. Leavis. This is Leavis in an essay on James as critic: 'A critic who would be intelligent about the novel must be intelligent about life: no discussion of the novel by any other kind of critic is worth attention'. D. H. Lawrence said, 'We judge a work of art by its effect on our sincere and vital emotion, and nothing else'.[4]

   In Leavis, the thoroughly influential critic of Anglo-Saxon criticism, we have a voice that refuses the idea of 'literary language', and denies that there can be merely 'literary' values. This is in opposition to Paterian ideas that the work of art can be judged as an aesthetic whole – as a thing of beauty in itself: for Leavis, a 'literary' text would be suspect. What Leavis looks for from poetic writing is rarely theorized: the language in some ways must enact its meaning, and it must not be some special language, but like Wordsworth's prescription of the 'language really used by men', be the language that tastes of lived experience, with muscle and body within it. (The requirements sound fairly Puritan, and not that far away from nineteenth century muscular Christianity.) Thus Leavis praises Gerard Manley Hopkins for being 'consciously bent on bringing back into poetry the life and strength of the living, the spoken language', adducing a letter of Hopkins: 'it seems to me that the poetical language of the age shd. be the current language heightened, to any degree heightened and unlike it, but not (I mean normally: passing freaks and graces are another thing) an obsolete one' (quoted from *The Common Pursuit* Chapter 3). Poetry should have the texture of the spoken voice, and there is no special language for a poet.

Go back on the non-Paterian quotations in this second section, as they define literature and criticism, and think what assumptions underlie them. Do common themes emerge in these assessments?

DISCUSSION

It is apparent how often the word *life* appears: in Arnold, James and in Leavis. It is assumed that literature has everything to do with 'felt life', and the term seems almost to imply something religious. So it would appear: for literature is becoming important precisely as the traditional appeals of religion are growing less (through Darwinism and scientific and philosophical scepticism). Note, related to that, the appeal to emotion, in Wordsworth and Lawrence: and there are, obviously, connections to be made between that term and 'life'. Thirdly, it seems that there is a strong appeal to the idea of spontaneity: the only room Coleridge has for style in composition is the idea of the best order of words: Wordsworth thinks that poetry comes 'naturally'; look at the implications of Lawrence's word 'sincere', and see how Leavis brushes aside the idea of mere 'professional' skills in criticism with the demand that intelligence about life is the only thing valuable. Above all, note the strong appeal to value judgements throughout – from 'best poetry' to 'best words', to 'vital emotion' (note the pun that underlies 'vital'? and Leavis' dismissal of any critic not intelligent about life.

This tradition of criticism clearly has no time for style, in contrast to Pater, or in the sense that Pope praised it, as being the adornment of subject-matter: Leavis holds that the poetic use of language (a formulation which he used to avoid having to designate any text in a purely formal way as poem, play or novel) is creative, generative of meaning. Practical criticism becomes an effort to show (a) that the writer has felt and knows personally and intimately the subject-matter written about, that to quote again George Eliot – a writer much admired by James, Lawrence and Leavis – 'the whole being' is involved in it; and (b) that the work of art grows spontaneously, with a deep 'animating intention', as Leavis put it. The work of art thus imposes its own rules as it grows organically, and it cannot be described abstractly, or in a formalist manner (e.g. the deployment of technical terms, such as I include in the appendix are of little value in discussion of poetry – indeed, deploying them absolves the critic from taking the measure of what the text has to say).

Arnold urged a 'real, not an historical estimate of poetry' and the tradition I have outlined has argued that a text was valuable in so far as it could speak to us in the here and now. With Donne (as opposed to Milton), Leavis writes in *Revaluation* (1936), 'we read on as we read the living'. Leavis would point to the dramatic openings of Donne's poems:

> I wonder, by my troth, what thou and I
> Did, till we loved?
>> ('The Good-morrow')

> Busy old fool, unruly sun,
> Why dost thou thus
> Through windows and through curtains call on us?
>> ('The Sunne Rising')

> For God's sake hold your tongue and let me love
>> ('The Canonization')

They are all openings that presume the speaker to be self-dramatizing, and belong within a dramatic situation, where you are to imagine the setting – a bedroom in the first two examples, and a place for an argument (a law-court, or a church), in the third. The kinship of Donne with Shakespeare is proclaimed by the way that these two contemporaries are so close to the idiom of the theatre; and Leavis' admiration for the 'immediacy' of the voice in poetry has its roots in the sense that Donne's poetry involves great flexibility of tone of voice. Henry James advised authors to 'dramatize, dramatize' every situation, (Preface (1907) to *The Altar of the Dead*) and Leavis takes this seriously in admiring the idea that there is a dramatic – hence individual, hence particular – voice at work in Donne's lyrics. The energy and burst of spirit in each of these quotations is evident, and in the first, Leavis comments on the playing-off of the regularity of the metrical line against the emphasized 'Did', which coming at the start of a line, after the enjambement (i.e. the run-on from line to line) gives the strong sense of a man in dialogue and pondering.

F. R. Leavis and Literary Language

Leavis, as Francis Mulhern points out in his *The Moment of Scrutiny*, (1979) is the critic whose influence has been dominant within British literary criticism this century; his sense of great books (those which provide a 'liberal education') has formed a powerful hegemony which has taken over even those in Britain deeply antagonistic to him. As suggested above, he had little time for the concept of the 'literary': and perhaps an interesting entry into his work on the subject of poetic language may be found in his essay on Keats in *Revaluation*. The essay needs to be seen in context, but he argues that Keats' development was bound up with his loss of a strain of self-conscious literariness derived from Spenser and Milton, poets both admired by Keats, but admired for a sonority, a canorous quality that forces a wedge between sound (admired for its own sake) and sense. Spenser certainly wrote in a determinedly 'literary language', opting in the *The Faerie Queen* (1590–96) for a then archaic, vaguely Chaucerian English. Keats imitated with interest

> Spenserian vowels that elope with ease,
> And float along like birds o'er summer seas.
> (Letter of September 1816)

and the delight in richness of texture of sound for its own sake is similarly a feature of poets who leaned on Keats: Tennyson, Hopkins, Wilfred Owen, for instance, the last of whom begins his poem 'Exposure', dealing with the 1914–18 War, and specifically with the Front in 1917, with

> Our brains ache, in the merciless iced east winds that knive us . . .

where a self-conscious literariness is obvious. Owen's poem aims for beauty, and the packed quality of three adjectives, with their assonance, and the verb 'knive' that reflects earlier uses of the 'i' sounds, as well as being stark as a choice of word in itself, is Keatsian enough. (The first three words echo the 'Ode to a Nightingale' – 'My heart aches . . .'.) The three adjectives reflect Keats' injunction to 'load every rift of [the] subject with ore' (letter to Shelley of August, 1820). A Leavis based – criticism would, I think, find the Owen too rich, too self-consciously beautiful, too much mere 'literary language'. I leave you to think about this.

Leavis concludes an exemplary piece of practical criticism on the 'Nightingale' Ode by saying that 'it is as if Keats were making major poetry out of minor' (*Revaluation*, p. 207). In other words, he sees the literariness as out of gear with the subject-matter, and imposing a nostalgic beauty and luxury upon it. Keats had to learn by losing what he called 'the false beauty proceeding from art', by rejecting 'Miltonic inversions' in poetry (specifically, *Hyperion*), for 'English ought to be kept up' (letter of 21 September 1819). Thus Leavis sees the importance of the later poetry to be that it is Shakespearian, (p. 215), and no longer 'decorative-descriptive' (p. 216). We can construct out of Leavis' reading of Keats his sense that Shakespeare is 'English' in a sense that the literary Spenser and Milton are not, and that instead of 'literary language', the use of a 'strong idiomatic naturalness, a racy vigour' (p. 25) associated with Shakespeare and Jonson is characteristic of 'Englishness' and of the highest poetic art.

The strong value-judgements, the ideology of a natural, spontaneous 'English' form of writing and speaking, are obvious in Leavis, and have incurred much criticism. Later, in Chapters 5 and 6, it may become clear how the opposition Leavis sets up between different types of writing may be collapsed. Yet it remains a point for discussion how far those discriminations are not actually fastening on very important differences within – admittedly – equally artificial modes of writing, and revelatory of contrasting ideological positions within which the poets worked: for example, the 'Englishness' that Leavis sets up, turns out to be often in the service of non-conformity, of non-subservience to established, conventional interests, while the Spenserian mode, with its simulacrum of learning and thus of sophistication (though I want to use different arguments about the Miltonic) certainly comes across, in its various manifestations, as politically reactionary, and safe. In thus distinguishing between modes of writing, it becomes apparent that deciding how to write involves choices which are more than stylistic. Each of Leavis's enthusiasms in poetry – Donne, Wordsworth, Hopkins, Eliot, Pound, for instance – have been marked by their forward-lookingness in moving away from fixed and clearly artificial verse-forms.

American New Criticism

The criticism discussed thus far, though it stressed texts should be read as though they had an immediate present existence, was always interested in putting literature into an historical context, but its American cousin goes the other way. *The New Criticism* was the title of a book by John Crowe Ransom in 1941, and it set out a position that owed something to Empson and Richards, but more to T. S. Eliot, who had argued, in 1919, in an essay on *Hamlet* for 'the objective correlative'. Eliot amplified the meaning of the phrase by saying that a literary work must find 'a set of objects, a situation, a chain of events, which shall be the formula of [a] *particular* emotion'.[5] In *Hamlet*, Eliot contended, this was missing; instead emotional problems boiled over from the author onto the play. Eliot is thus arguing for the work of art to be self-contained, separate from its author, existing in a world of its own. In another essay of 1919, 'Tradition and the Individual Talent', he argued for the total separation in writing and criticism of the artist from the man: the 'man who suffers' from 'the mind that creates'.

With such a doctrine as this, the New Critics, who included Cleanth Brooks, R. P. Blackmur, Allen Tate, René Wellek and Austin Warren, contended for a view that has become very influential: that the work of art – particularly the poem, the focus of attention of the new critics – must be considered as an object, apart from history, and apart from the intentions of the author: to judge the work in the light of them is to commit what W. K. Wimsatt and M. C. Beardsley called 'the intentionalist fallacy'. They described this in *The Verbal Icon* (1954): the title is relevant indeed, for it suggests the way in which a poem may be viewed: as a complete artefact. Cleanth Brooks had already written *The Well Wrought Urn* (1947): again, this (almost literally) puts poetry on a pedestal, and suggests that it must be looked at as an artefact existing in terms of its form, and in terms of its unity: this last word being a central stress for Coleridge: that the work of art built up to an organic whole.

The American New Critics do, indeed, evoke the idea of a 'literary language'. I. A. Richards distinguished between *scientific* or *referential* language, and *poetic* or *emotive*. He saw a split between a scientific and an aesthetic view of the world, and drew on Coleridge's sense – crucial to the New Critics – that poetry evokes in the reader a 'poetic faith', which consists in a 'willing suspension of disbelief' (*Biographia Literaria* Ch. 14). In other words, the actual literal truth-content of the poem does not matter – Coleridge is talking about 'The Ancient Mariner', and no one believes that what the Mariner describes actually took place. But an appropriate reading of the poem would, for Coleridge, accept that the poem was dealing with things that were true in some spiritual way, and would be so absorbed by the poem anyway that the 'scientific' validity of it would not be relevant.

In the New Critics, this sense that poetry taps a level of meaning that is purely to do with emotions and not to do with scientific fact, encourages a close look at the work of its form, especially its 'economy of form' – something that Henry James praised: no excess, no great length. The text's rhythm, its imagery, its use of symbolism, its reconciliation of opposite points of view in a hierarchy of meanings, and its ability to build up a self-contained world – these are crucial markers for American New Critics. The tradition has persisted, especially with Paul de Man, Hillis Miller, Geoffrey Hartman – names associated with American 'deconstruction' – with the appropriation of Derrida's work in the States. We shall return to Derrida, and to De Man, much later.

At this point, I suggest you consider the English and American traditions discussed, and note the similarities and the differences. Above all, what difficulties do you see in either of the positions?

DISCUSSION

Similarities The stress on close reading; on the sense that the text can be approached in an Aristotelian, empirical manner; examining simply the words on the page is common. Poetry (this is more true of New Criticism), is favoured over the novel; a tight-knit structure which can be looked at in detail is preferred to novelistic narrative. Henry James in the Preface to *The Tragic Muse* called the novels of Dickens and Tolstoy 'loose baggy monsters'. This lesser place given to the novel means that there is a strong ideology that the poem has to do with 'the human condition', with permanent values: novels are, of course, through being set in time, much more committed to historical matters and to change. A novel does not work like a verbal icon. Note, too, that there is a strong commitment to the view that literature can be defined in terms of depth. Ordinary language that says what it means is rejected in favour of 'ambiguity' (Empson), 'paradox' (Brooks), 'ambivalence', and richness of imagery and of metaphor. The implications of this in terms of class and education should be obvious. Popular culture is not worth looking at because it does not invest in depth. Above all, however, the shared assumption is that there is something almost metaphysical about the existence of the complete work. It has its own 'intention', which goes beyond the views of the author, who is not, therefore, the best judge of what has been written. 'Never trust the artist, trust the tale' is a demand of D. H. Lawrence's, in his *Studies in Classic American Literature*,[6] suggesting that the artist's intended moral or meaning becomes deformed by the autonomy of the work of art.

Differences   The main separation between the two is in the place given to value judgement in the British tradition. American New Criticism hardly moves out of the poem back to the real world: the two worlds are not continuous, and the interest in the structure of the poem leads to a type of analysis best described as 'formalist': concerned with observing the details of the poem and describing these faithfully. (We will look at the Russian Formalists in the next chapter.) Leavis' criticism was much more interested in the connections of literature to history, and thus to sociological and non-textual matters. The affective, emotional quality of the poem was enough for the American new critic.

Difficulties   There are three areas that I would want to isolate immediately:
1   The suggestion, in Leavis, as in others, that there is no 'literary' language in the works dealt with: that there is something profoundly natural, or 'real' – a favourite Leavis term – in the successful work. But a moment's reflection should suggest a weakness here. To be natural is the effect of art: to write (a non-natural activity) in 'language such as men do use' as Wordsworth urged in the *Preface* is

(a) to be non-natural by making a necessary selection; and (b) to have to create the effect of naturalness. Scriptwriters for soap operas know that if you recorded what people actually said at the breakfast table, you wouldn't have a script at all. To write a scene that sounds as though it was a depiction of a typical breakfast scene is an achievement of art: in this case, the art that conceals art. Supposing Wordsworth had really written down what Cumberland peasants said. It certainly wouldn't have been the *Lyrical Ballads*. The implications of this point seem crucial. Instead of Romantic spontaneity, we are left with the idea that literature is actually a matter of rhetorical devices. If neither Donne nor Milton uses the speaking voice in poetry, what happens to the distinction between them that Leavis makes in suggesting that Milton uses something like an artificial language?

2   There is no room given for the reader in this criticism. It is assumed that s/he is a competent reader of the language; knows how to take an image, metaphor, and so on, and, with the benefit of teaching, should have no difficulty in coping with a text perhaps 400 years old. Again, reflection will suggest that no such reader exists, except on the basis of the circular argument that a competent reader is someone who reads like the critic. Doctor Johnson spoke of 'the common reader'. Perhaps such a homogenous group existed in the mid-eighteenth century, when the reading public was limited anyway, but it is questionable whether it exists today, except as the result of a special education – such as reading English at a college or university. There, training in 'literary language' effectively 'naturalizes' such terms as image, simile, metaphor, etc. and makes students and teachers think that to understand them is a process that comes easily, and above all as a matter of commonsense, whereas it comes about as a result of a specific sort of education. Since the reader is left out, with only the assumption that if s/he reads properly, s/he will come to the same kind of sense of the text that the critic has, there is no room for the point that understanding a text depends on one's place in history, that there cannot be an absolute fixed meaning of a text. If meaning is available like that, all historical, all educational, all class and gender differences are made to disappear.

3   There is the assumption that texts mean what they say. Art is a matter of communication, between the writer (or the text in New Criticism), and the reader – who is, as said before, hardly presumed to exist save as someone who can catch the finely nuanced meanings that are conveyed in a text. In later chapters, we shall consider the impact of both Freudian psychoanalysis and of Derrida's deconstruction on this point of view. In the meantime, it seems enough to note that the assumption that there can be a simple – or perhaps

complex – meaning puts an intolerable burden on the artist, who is presumed to have meant in a deep sense many of the complexities of the text, and it assumes that meanings themselves transcend history; that we can know something of what Donne meant. Though there is plenty of room in all this criticism for the autonomy of the work of art, and for the appearance of non-intended meanings, there is still the assumption that these meanings all add up to something: to a unity, by which one preferred meaning comes through. Empson, with his stress on the ambiguities that are inherent in language may be thought of as a partial exception to this principle.

The exercise of close reading of specific texts, of 'the words on the page' makes the assumption that the text can be looked at in its own right: how from this approach could the irony be perceived, for instance, that Duck, complaining of owner landlords could use no other poetic language than that of the polite and to him oppressive society – of Pope, of course, to make his poetic attack in? And has not the division of poetic language into two categories – that where its local life can be examined in great detail and that where it cannot, created a false sense of literature? (Can this viewpoint really cope with oral, as opposed to written poetry, for example? – since oral poetry cannot use the same kind of ambiguity, of richness of form that a later poetry can.) Ballads, folksongs, popular lyrics, all these seem to be marginalized by this technique. Literature gets a strong narrowing definition from this method of reading.

However convinced you are by these criticisms, or 'difficulties' or by the approaches outlined here, they are clearly issues which we will have to have to continue to focus on in following chapters. Before going further, therefore, it is important to have an overall sense of what is at stake in the traditions presented here, and you may wish to go back for another look before going on.

3. Modernism and Formalism

The goal of literary work (or literature as work) is to make the reader
no longer a consumer, but a producer of the text.

Roland Barthes: *S/Z*

In the Anglo-American tradition I have discussed, questions of
theory are subordinated to an empirical approach which assumes
that you can always start by looking at the words on the page.
Though there is a theory at work, clearly, it has been left implicit
only. In this chapter, however, the conscious question whether there
is a literary kind of language becomes more central. Views that
suggest there is something of an 'essential' transcending value in
poetry itself will find the approach less sympathetic: I am thinking of
Gerard Manley Hopkins saying that 'rhetoric is the common and
teachable part of literature' (Letter of 7 August, 1886); suggesting
that poetry itself is a mysterious, unnameable quality; or Robert
Frost defining poetry as 'that which gets lost from verse in translation'; or the American poet Archibald MacLeish's epigram, 'A
poem must not mean, / But be'. But perhaps these definitions, which
suggest that there is something irreducible about poetry or prose
writing when it is 'literature', are guilty of a kind of ahistoricalism:
they take no account of changes which affect the production of
literature, or, indeed, of the idea that texts are produced through
historical circumstances at all.

  In contrast, take the work of Roland Barthes, (1915–1980) the
French critic, and of his early work, *Writing degree zero* (1952), a
brilliant study of changes in French literature centred on the dates
1650, 1789, 1848, 1850, and drawing on the work of the Hungarian
Marxist critic, Georg Lukács. Briefly, Barthes' argument is that the
years around 1650 saw the emergence of French 'classical' writing,
where there was a common view of how to express sentiment in
literary language. The French Revolution of 1789 threw this into

difficulty as the bourgeoisie asserted their hegemony in the place of the *ancien régime*, and proved, by 1848, that they could be as reactionary as the power that they had displaced. The novelist of the corruption of the bourgeoisie was Balzac: his death in 1850, two years later, makes a significant divide. Flaubert, on the other side of the divide, with *Madame Bovary*, (1857) makes the change. 'Around 1850', Barthes writes, 'classical writing . . . disintegrated, and the whole of literature, from Flaubert to the present day, became the problematics of writing'. What is implied here is that Flaubert's writing becomes a retreat into itself, away from engagement with the bourgeois world, and obsessed from then on with ways of renewing language in a mode that was not itself bourgeois. Merely writing a realist novel was no longer an option – rather, as Barthes puts it, 'writing is a blind alley, and it is because society itself is a blind alley'.[1]

Now this opens up a discussion that few of the critics of the last chapter took any cognizance of at all. Flaubert's interest in 'style' begins a process of separation between the textual and the 'real' world: it is no longer assumed straightforwardly that the text describes the world. The distinction, discussed in the last chapter, that was made by I. A. Richards between two types of language becomes possible as French symbolist poetry announces that 'all the world exists to be made into a book' (Mallarmé),[2] and thus privileges the poetic world over the real, commonsense one. 'You don't write poems with ideas, you write them with words' was Mallarmé's reply to a poet stuck with the difficulty of setting down his ideas. Above all, language is forced to its limits, becomes difficult – as T. S. Eliot said in 1921, 'poetry for our time must be difficult'.[3]

I said this view of style was foreign to most of the critics in the Anglo-American tradition, but of course, there are exceptions: in Pater and in Wilde, for instance. Pater's alliance of art with music has strong affiliations with Mallarmé's sense that a poem is non-referential, is not *about* anything, and Flaubert's influence on Wilde, Joyce, Woolf and indeed on Pound and Eliot is important.

Let us look at a case in point, the following poem, published in 1923, by the American writer Wallace Stevens (1879–1955) who in his poem 'Man carrying thing' said 'poetry must resist the intelligence almost successfully', and in 'The man with the blue guitar' makes the very Modernist statement that 'poetry is the subject of the poem'. What evidence is there here, in this poem, called 'Anecdote of the Jar', that 'the subject of the poem' is not something outside the poem? You may wish to consider such questions as: rhyme, structure, repetition of words or sounds, rather than questions about the content.

I placed a jar in Tennessee,
And round it was, upon a hill.
It made the slovenly wilderness
Surround that hill.

The wilderness rose up to it
And sprawled around, no longer wild.
The jar was round upon the ground
And tall and of a port in air.

It took dominion everywhere.
The jar was gray and bare.
It did not give of bird or bush,
Like nothing else in Tennessee.

DISCUSSION

The pattern or structure of the poem seems interesting. To take the rhyming is a good way to start: it begins unrhymed though it rhymes 'hill' with 'hill', but by lines 8–10 that has changed, and there is a triple rhyme – air/where/bare. (Just as with that triple rhyme in the Duck poem?) And then it goes back to an unrhymed couplet. But the last word is the same as the last word of the first line – 'Tennessee'. So that the poem completes itself without doing so in an obvious way. And the triple rhyme has been prepared for, with the internal rhyme that came in line 7 – round/ground. And that steadying, centrally balanced line picks up other references to 'round', in lines 2, 4 and 6. So that roundness looks like a central figure or trope that the poem develops; as it comes back to the first line at the end, and as it starts again, having gone right round, in the last two lines. And roundness is, of course, the shape of the jar.

The structure describes the poem. It takes dominion everywhere: rhymes breed rhymes: look at gray/bare. Is it enough to describe it as a verbal pattern, to say it is 'about' nothing, only 'about' itself?

You might add to that a sense of playfulness. Why Tennessee? I suspect it's only in for the shape of the word, two 'n's, two 's's and four 'e's. And the title – 'Anecdote of the jar' suggests someone telling you a story perhaps over a drink. To 'go for a jar' is to have a drink. Perhaps Stevens is playing on the idea that the poet is drunk with inspiration – as at the end of Coleridge's 'Kubla Khan'. And what about the double negative in the last two lines? Do they really negate anything? 'I didn't do nothing' – did the speaker do anything, or not? Does not a double negative often affirm something strongly?

It might be possible to argue, on the basis of Stevens' known interest in the imagination and its power to change reality, that the jar is art, and the wilderness is nature: which would make the poem referential, discussing a philosophical problem; but would that help with 'slovenly'? Or with 'a port in air' – does 'air' mean 'bearing', the way you carry yourself (the French verb *porter* is 'to carry')? And how much does it fit the tone?

There are questions of subjective reaction here. Further, the poem leads straight into the New Critical position where a separation is made between poetic and scientific language: indeed, it has gone beyond, for this poetic language is not even referential in any straightforward way. While the poem may be a 'verbal icon', 'a machine made with words', as the poet Louis Zukovsky called it, its difference from that critical position is that while the poem does exist complete in a self-enclosed world, it is also sufficient to see it as not pointing outside itself: as being nothing but writing: to try to say that the jar symbolizes this, or the wilderness that, is both unnecessary and slightly absurd.

This Modernist poem suggests there is nothing beyond the text. That is, the perception of reality is ultimately effected through language: the world out there cannot be known except through language: and language itself is not innocent, but highly coloured, loaded with strong assumptions which have been taken for granted. That was the issue faced by the post-1850 novelists and poets, according to Barthes; and in philosophical terms, it has been the major preoccupation of the twentieth century; Wittgenstein was the most important exponent of the view that all philosophical problems have a linguistic origin, and that 'philosophy is a battle against the bewitchment of our intelligence by means of language' (*Philosophical Investigations*, no. 109). Indeed, Wittgenstein belongs to the moment of Modernism himself, in that he makes 'a radical break with the idea that language always functions in one way, always serves the same purpose: to convey thoughts' (*Investigations* no. 304). Language does not simply serve communication: indeed, the question is to what extent communication is possible at all through language. I am not just thinking of the surprising number of ways statements can be read, deliberately, or non-deliberately: as where BILL STICKERS WILL BE PROSECUTED used to appear as police notices on walls in the East End of London, and people would write beneath BILL STICKERS IS INNOCENT. In day-to-day utterance, the possibility of non-understanding is limited, though it happens. The context, the signs we make, the lack of other possibilities inherent in the situation cuts down the number of mistakes possible. In conceptual utterance, to what extent communication takes place between people is often definitely questionable.

The consequences for writing of the position outlined in Barthes need examining. He draws attention to language itself as the opaque medium that cannot be escaped from: to 'the prison house of language', (a phrase actually from Nietzsche, and the book title of a work by the American Marxist critic Fredric Jameson on just this topic) – the idea that language can prevent thought rather than facilitate it, since it binds the speaker/writer to fixed ways of thinking and of perceiving. Further, implicit in Lukács and Barthes and other Marxist critics is the view that especially in the second half of the nineteenth century, poetic language, and that used for creative writing generally, has become the property of a hegemonic class that tries to monopolize thought in its own interests, and that indeed, does so – using the category of 'literature', constituted as an academic subject, to define preferred modes of thought.

The perception of a crisis within language at the beginning of the twentieth century prompted two related alternative ways forward to be made. One was to accept that language by its ability to name and misname actually controls perception, and to attempt to get away from that into a near-private world where language is used differently and non-referentially – indeed in a 'literary' way. The other was to try to deform the traditional uses of language in the attempt to force a new mode of perception. The first leads to the charge of aestheticism, of preoccupation with style, and disengagement from life and political reality. And the need to make poetry difficult brings in a law of diminishing returns. The harder a text becomes, the less it will be read, except by professional readers – students and academics. Modernism produced violent assaults on conventional language uses. The Russian Futurists – Khlebnikov (1885–1922) and Mayakovsky (1893–1930) – demanded the 'depoeticized word', 'zaum', a 'transrational language', and made the bourgeois jump with their 1912 Manifesto, *A slap in the face of public taste*. The Italian Futurist Marinetti (1876–1944), who demanded 'words at liberty' from grammatical and syntactic order, drew attention by his arrangement of words on the page to their graphic and sound qualities, as things in themselves. These were attempts to break the mould of the attachment of the word to bourgeois ideology; but of course, the Futurist movement was ambiguous politically: Marinetti moved towards Fascism, Mayakovsky towards Marxism.

What is, however, evident from all this is that language has become the central issue in Modernist thought (from roughly about the turn of the century) and beyond, towards the present. An example of the work of a particular group of Modernists, the Russian Formalists, is worth turning to, therefore.

Russian Formalism

In 1917, the twenty-four year old Victor Shklovsky, a member of the then new Moscow Linguistic group, produced a polemical essay, *Art as Technique*, which set out a new position on the function of art. His argument was that poetic language works by its use of *ostranenie*, 'defamiliarization', which removes objects from 'the automization of perception', and does so by forcing new perception, 'deforming' language, 'making it new' (to quote Pound again), 'making strange'. It may not be an exaggeration to suggest that discussion of 'literary language' begins here, for Shklovsky belonged with critics who included Roman Jakobson, Yury Tynanov, Boris Eichenbaum, Boris Tomashevsky, Vladimir Propp, Osip Brik, and had Mikhail Bakhtin on the sidelines. In Petersburg, there was an equivalent group, called *Opoyaz*, an acronym for the 'society for the study of literary language', founded in 1916, a year after the Moscow group. 'Formalism' was to last through the 1920s, when it was effectively removed from the Russian scene. In Prague, it surfaced again as the Prague Linguistic circle, after 1926, where Jakobson was influential.

The inspiration behind Formalism was the sense that the issue of language itself was crucial. The 'realist' novel assumed that there could be a way of simply mirroring the world; the Formalists objected that this view took no account of language itself as a coloured and colouring medium, but assumed that its terms of reference were natural, and not the products of particular cultural formations and particular cultural histories. When people complain in the *Daily Telegraph*, as they do frequently, that Standard English is under threat, they are speaking for the claims of a particular register of language to wield hegemonic control over everyone's ways of thinking: but Standard English is itself something that serves the interests of a conservative middle class very well. Examples of the way that language is itself a site for contest are obvious: think of the implications of 'manpower'; 'chairman'; 'man' (as in *The Ascent of Man*); 'his' as a general pronoun; think of the differences between the way Tories referred to the 'Greenham Common ladies', and their naming themselves the 'Greenham Common women'; think of the differences between the word 'gay' and 'queer', and the power of naming racial groups as 'coloured', as though 'white' were not a colour. In literature, language so familiarizes that it makes the products of culture seem natural, and a 'realist' novelist such as Tolstoy works to prevent the reader from thinking that what they are looking at is a *discourse*, an artificially contrived way of signifying. Instead, they are to think that here is a complex vision of life, which is simply observed faithfully. Russian Formalism began as an attempt to disengage the study of 'literariness' from other forms of writing, such as biography or history: criticism had the function of showing that literature was marked out by devices, techniques (of which 'realism' is one) that gave it its distinctiveness. Rather than just accepting the authority of the text and its author, and commenting on the vision within the work, it insisted that critical work began by looking at the literary devices by which the vision was articulated. It had the task of showing that art was a discursive practice, and that its modes of working needed to be shown.

Thus, in writing about Tolstoy, Shklovsky fastened on those places where there was a 'seeing things out of their normal context'. In *Kholstomer*, a Tolstoyan novella, private property is presented, and criticized from the point of view of a horse, and so 'defamiliarized'. Elsewhere, battles are described as if they were something new: the reader is thus made to see afresh. These are places where Tolstoy made evident his own literariness, rather than presenting himself as a realist novelist. At such moments, there was a 'foregrounding' of the literary device; attention was switched from what was said to how it was said. 'Foregrounding' was a concept implicit with the Formalists, but adopted fully by the Prague circle: Jan Mukarovsky, a member of that group, was to say that 'the function of poetic language' – he is distinguishing it from standard speech – 'consists in the maximum foregrounding of the utterance . . . it is not used in the services of communication, but in order to place in the foreground the act of expression, the act of speech itself'.[4] It is worth comparing this idea of 'foregrounding' with some comments of T. S. Eliot in his essay called 'Philip Massinger' on the seventeenth-century dramatists, contemporaries of Shakespeare, whose style influenced him greatly: 'these lines of Tourneur and of Middleton exhibit that perpetual slight alteration of language, words perpetually juxtaposed in new and sudden combinations, meanings perpetually *eingeschachtelt* [one meaning put into a box within another] into meanings, which evidences a very high development of the senses'. The perception, akin to that of the Formalists, is of writers 'foregrounding' certain aspects of their writing, with the view of 'defamiliarizing' the reader.

So too, Shklovsky called Lawrence Sterne's eighteenth-century novel *Tristram Shandy* the most typical novel in world literature; by this he meant that Sterne's text, which never disguises its techniques of working, but draws attention to its digressions, to the whole artificiality of telling a story, and to the various tricks that have to be resorted to in order to make the telling seem right, just shows openly what other novels conceal – its various devices. Sterne plays with the reader so that the time taken to relate something accords with the actual time it would take for the thing related to happen: it is crucial here for us to remember that the 'novel' as an art-form is closely connected in its appearance to the emergence of a strong sense of linear time. There is no equivalent sense of time in, say, *Othello*. Sterne does things all novelists do; the book parodies standard novelistic devices, laying them bare: something the Modernist text also does.

The Formalists were anti-bourgeois, in that sense belonging to the moment of the Russian Revolution, and antagonistic to middle-class perceptions being made natural through nineteenth-century fiction. Their theoretical sense was fed by the implications of the work of the linguist Saussure (1857–1913), whose *Course in General Linguistics* (published posthumously in 1914, from lecture notes taken by his students, and to be discussed later), had shown how language was not to be considered as something natural and inherently meaningful, but rather constructed, allowing certain things to be said, as well as preventing certain others from being articulated. At the same time, they were interested in pure form as the way to the pure aesthetic experience. Aesthetics – the study of the beautiful – had been treated by Kant, who in *The Critique of Judgment* (1790) had declared aesthetic pleasure to be realized most fully through art, which had 'purposiveness without purpose', which was 'pure' and not applied or in any way utilitarian, and which demanded 'disinterestedness' from the perceiver. The Formalists opened themselves to the charge that in accepting the category of the aesthetic they were ignoring content, that they were caught in a trap where they had to make an absolute category out of literature. The similarity with later American New Criticism is worth considering. At times they stressed only the autonomy of the work of art, and ignored its historical production.

Indeed, it could be argued that their radicalism would have been better served by a removal of the term 'literariness' as that which made the text into art: as it was, they perpetuated a term and a concept that might be seen as encouraging the view that there was a definite body of writings called 'literature'. And the effect of it was the searching out of qualities that would make a text 'literary'.

Thus Roman Jakobson, in *The New Russian Poetry* (1919), while praising the Russian Futurists, such as the Brecht-like Mayakovsky, and using Khlebnikov in his analyses, played down poetry as communication: saw it rather as 'the realm of emotion and spiritual experience', and the study of literature was to be 'the study of literariness'. Here is the isolation of the concept of 'literary language': Jakobson's interest was in 'the device' by which the writer enforces on the reader a new awareness of reality. By 1920, Jakobson had left Moscow for Prague, but the sense of the need to put literary language on a firm, positivist basis, remained. Tynanov, another of the group, isolated each specific literary movement in terms of its 'dominants' – i.e. those elements that controlled its linguistic form; Osip Brik, in *Rhythm and Syntax* (1927), stressed the importance of sound repetition in poetry as crucial: rather than stressing images and metaphors, he talked in terms of 'orchestration', of sound-quality as that which the writer manipulates. Repeated sounds, the number of repetitions, the order in which sounds follow each other in repeated groups, and the position of sounds in rhythmical units all become important, and make terms like 'assonance' and 'rhyme' very amateurish. (Rhyme, indeed, is just one part of sound-repetition.) Tomashevsky's work was done on prose, discussing the distinction between the 'fable' – the story – and the narrative structure; (Propp had already studied, in his work on the Russian folk tale, the thirty-one possible narrative functions that permit narrative to go forwards in the hundred folk tales he discussed). Common to all this work is its exposure of the 'device' that structures literary work, but which is conventionally concealed so that it all appears to be natural.

At this point, I want to develop the comparison between Russian Formalism and American New Criticism, and make a preliminary assessment of the Formalists' position.
1   The crucial similarity between the two groups is the interest in the text without historical back-ups: the text is there, but it functions perhaps in different ways. For the Formalists, its method of signifying is crucial: for the New Critics, it is interpretation. But both groups would separate the text firmly from context, or commentary.
2   The radical nature of the Formalists is worth contrasting with the political conservatism (often a product of the deep South area they came from) of the New Critics. In the Formalists' case, the necessity is for deviation from the norm, from standard speech, and they drew on the distinction Saussure had made between *la langue* and *la parole* – the first term implying the whole range of conventional language, and the second the individual speech-act – to suggest that the *parole* – the individual poem – must separate itself clearly from the normal, bourgeois-controlled *langue*. The New Critics, in strong contrast, tended to cling to the work of art as the only bastion of values left in the modern world!
3   There is a big difference, too, in the attempt the Formalists made to be scientific about language. Formalism tried to make 'literary language' something that could be measured and known objectively. Shklovsky divided up Sherlock Holmes stories into nine narrative

units that never altered, effectively, from tale to tale (I have mentioned Propp as doing the same with traditional folk-tales, as also, much later of course, Umberto Eco, the Italian professor of semiotics, did with the James Bond novels). Metrics became important with Brik and Eichenbaum, in order to assess how a poem was literary. Similarly, Eichenbaum was interested in the study of rhetoric for getting at poetic styles. Now in doing this, they effectively eliminated the metaphysical idea of the poem as something 'irreducible' in analysis, the product of 'life', as Leavis argued.

Yet how scientific was all this? Could it not also be said that it was a metaphysical activity to try to identify a 'literary language', for they assumed that a text could be described in some absolute sense as 'literary'? They accepted that 'literariness' exists from age to age, untroubled by history. They took no account of the argument that the concept of literature is *produced*, by historical and cultural determinants, nor did they attend to the very basic question why some texts come to be singled out as literature.

What remains clear about Russian Formalism is that its definition of what to look for in literary language remains very restricted. Jakobson's sense that what is to be studied is literariness, rather than content, is austere; and the contrast with Mikhail Bakhtin in this, as also in the 'scientific' sense of language he adopted, is strong.

The Novel and Heteroglossia

I have mentioned Saussure's distinction between *langue* and *parole*. The first of these terms refers to the range of linguistic possibilities open at one time to a speaker or writer. The second refers to the individual speech act of the person who uses the *langue*. Shklovsky and Jakobson were interested in how an individual text could, by its 'device', move away from the traditional and static thinking embodied in the *langue* to create a new *parole* – a text that would deform the standard thinking and speech that surrounded the poem. Saussure argued that attention must be paid to the *langue*: to the conditions of speech and thought out of which the *parole* emerged. Traditional criticism, of the type discussed in the last chapter, is of course, much more interested in thinking about the individual text that the poet or novelist has produced, and tends to treat it in isolation.

Bakhtin, influenced by Formalism and yet not quite associated with it, comes in here as a possible bridge between the two kinds of position outlined. During his lifetime he published, in 1929, *Problems of Dostoevsky's Poetics*, under his own name, – as well, it seems, as books under the names of colleagues, V. N. Volosinov and

P. N. Medvedev. In 1940, he finished a Ph.D. thesis, rejected at the
time, on Rabelais, eventually published in the Soviet Union in 1965.
At the end of his life, in 1975, four essays were collected into a work
translated as *The Dialogic Imagination*. It was a challenging career,
and not least because Bakhtin's effort was directed at emphasizing such concepts as 'polyphony', 'heteroglossia', 'dialogism' and
'reaccentuation'. Each of these terms resists definition, mainly
because each functions, really, as an anti-concept; each suggests the
possibility of dual, plural meaning.

Like the Formalists, Bakhtin talks about literary language, but
the effect of his work is to challenge the simple division between
langue and *parole*, and to suggest that the idea of a single deviation
from the *langue* is too simple, not doing justice to the way language
works. Everything is, potentially, double, in the sign-system that is
language: everything can be 'accentuated' in numbers of ways, and
be made to yield plural meanings. He discusses, particularly, the
novel, but that genre-term is his way of describing any text which has
elements of multi-accentuation in it, or polyphony, or many-
voicedness, anything that in its 'heteroglossia' challenges a 'mon-
ologic' or single voice speaking. For Bakhtin, the point is not that a
novel moves towards a unity, as it would have to do for the
Romantics or New Critics, but that it affirms plurality, that it cannot
be tied down to one preferred meaning. And this is because in the
novel, the text is always at the intersection of several signifying
systems: it contains different voices.

Jakobson tried to define a single literary element that makes a
text poetic, making it an individual *parole*. Bakhtin argues, in *The
Dialogic Imagination* (p. 308), that 'it is precisely the diversity of
speech, and not the unity of a normative shared language, that is the
ground of style'. That presentation of literary language succeeds his
discussion of passages of Dickens' *Little Dorrit*.

Let us look at an example of this. Before reading Bakhtin's
commentary, consider the tone(s) of voice of the passage (ignore the
fact that Bakhtin has put some of it into italics), the attitude of the
speaking voice, and the type of voice that it is – who is speaking? In
what follows, I will discuss both the passage itself, for its range of
voices, and Bakhtin on it.

> The conference was held at four or five o'clock in the afternoon, when
> all the region of Harley Street, Cavendish Square, was resonant of
> carriage-wheels and double-knocks. It had reached this point when
> Mr Merdle came home *from his daily occupation of causing the
> British name to be more and more respected in all parts of the civilised
> globe capable of appreciation of wholewide commercial enterprise
> and gigantic combinations of skill and capital*. For, though nobody

knew with the least precision what Mr Merdle's business was, except that it was to coin money, these were the terms in which everybody defined it on all ceremonious occasions, and which it was the last new polite reading of the parable of the needle's eye to accept without inquiry.

> *Little Dorrit*. 1.ch.33. (NB – the Oxford Dickens reads 'worldwide' for 'wholewide'.)

The italicized portion represents a parodic stylization of the language of ceremonial speeches (in parliaments and at banquets). The shift into this style is prepared for by the sentence's construction, which from the beginning is kept within bounds by a somewhat ceremonious epic tone. Further on – and already in the language of the author (and consequently in a different style) – the parodic meaning of the ceremoniousness of Merdle's labours becomes apparent: such a characterization turns out to be 'another's speech', to be taken only in quotation marks ('these were the terms in which everybody defined it on all ceremonious occasions').

Thus the speech of another is introduced into the author's discourse (the story) in *concealed form*, that is, without any of the *formal* markers usually accompanying such speech in the same 'language' – it is another's utterance in a language that is itself 'other' to the author as well, in the archaicized language of oratorical genres associated with hypocritical official celebrations.[5]

> *The Dialogic Imagination*, trans. Caryl Emerson and Michael Holquist, (Austin, Texas, 1981) p. 303.

DISCUSSION

Bakhtin has identified in this paragraph of Dickens three styles:

1   The mock-heroic opening: note the dehumanization here: people coming to Mr Merdle's house are turned into sounds only – of carriage wheels and double knocks. In effect there is no person there – just as, later in the book, Mr Merdle's fortune turns out to be non-existent.

2   The italicized portion – which Bakhtin sees as a parody of ceremonial speeches, taking his hint from 'these were the terms'.

3   The language of the author, which comments on the above, fairly cynically.

Is it possible to do more work on that third section? For example, in 'Mr Merdle's business . . . was to coin money', are we hearing an authorial comment, or the voice of the various people who fawn on Mr Merdle in their more frank private moments? (Would they say it to his face?) Much of the style of this paragraph is indeed 'high ceremonious' in character, but then we drop into the different diction of 'to coin money', which is definitely 'low' and non-epic: there is a plurality of voices introduced there. And what about the reference to Matthew 19, verses 23–24 – 'It is easier for a camel to go through the eye of a needle, than for a rich man to enter into the kingdom of God'? Why has that register been brought in? There seems to be an attitude to the Church, where there are also 'ceremonious occasions', for the Church's sense of the acceptability of wealth is insinuated here. In fact the syntax of that last part is quite puzzling. It seems to mean that 'to accept without asking where Mr Merdle got his money from was to collude in the new way of understanding the Biblical parable'. But it also seems to mean that there are *two* readings available of the parable: the polite and the impolite, and the 'polite' belongs to 'ceremonious occasions' and involves 'no inquiry': while the impolite would ask where Merdle's money came from; and *neither* reading, of course, has anything to do with the sense of the actual parable, which stands here in order to judge the morality and the reading-powers of the people involved. (The rich may get through the door in Harley Street, where Merdle lives, but they won't get through the door of Heaven.)

The language mocks ceremonious occasions: who would really say that Merdle's *occupation* was to make the British name more respected? That might be a result, a side-effect of his work (he is, in fact, a swindler), but it could not be called the immediate intention. The language draws attention to the displacements involved in people's speech: ceremonious occasions are the method by which the truth is displaced, not revealed. Note how the language of ceremony is also financial – 'appreciation' works as a pun.

It might be possible too, to go further than Bakhtin by questioning whether the 'author's voice' is heard at all: is not the voice of the narrator a projection, an adopted style – that of a *persona*, so that what the actual Dickens thought is not available to us, and indeed, of little interest?

What may seem puzzling is Bakhtin's reference to 'the other'. He contends that all speech is marked by the presence of the other: all speech is dialogic, containing the other person's language, tone, *timbre* in it: only on that basis is it possible to speak to anyone else at all. In the face of attempts from the Formalists to make a science out of detecting 'literariness', Bakhtin suggests that texts subvert any unitary way of taking them: they are already dual.

Bakhtin's argument implies that the wealth of voices heard even in this short paragraph of *Little Dorrit* implies the breakdown of the *langue/parole* distinction: Dickens is not writing out of one *langue* but out of several, and the text reveals a plurality of voices that prevent any one mode of discourse from becoming dominant. On this definition, 'literary language' is the sum total of all the voices from different traditions that the writer can interweave into the text. The result is equally important for those who would insist on a dogmatic way of understanding reality in one way (Stalinism seems to be the target), or those who would say that a tale or a narrative can be simply broken down into the sum of its structures (Propp, and the later 'structuralists'), and those who argue simply for the view that the text must exhibit some deliberate device that makes it literary, and lifts it above conventional utterance. Further, the view subverts the sense that the nineteenth-century realist novel is the voice of a dominant class, the bourgeoisie, for it suggests that the text can be re-accentuated: read differently, since it can contain no one single viewpoint.

The 'dialogic' and heteroglossic voice is heard strongly and obviously in Modernist texts such as Joyce, Eliot, Pound, Kafka, or Beckett: the text is a play of voices. Whereas Coleridgean or Leavisian criticism insisted on the literary text as whole, entire, Bakhtin's criticism draws attention to the etymology of the word: a text is a tissue, a weaving together of different strands, and to look for a single animating intention or deep vision within such a web limits the very language it is written in. Bakhtin's approach goes along with certain strains in Derrida, which will be returned to: at the moment, it is worth stressing how it illustrates the shortcomings both of Formalism and of the Anglo-Saxon tradition. Yet Bakhtin's sense of the novel as the subversion of genres, of attempts to fix and formalize language in use in a text, might be considered by criticism in the Leavis tradition to be a valuable ally in its rejection of theorized approaches, its insistence on the richness of the text.

Summary

In ways hardly guessed at by the writers and critics discussed in the last chapter, the European Modernists – including Kafka, Proust, Joyce, Beckett, Thomas Mann, Robert Musil, and so on – have stressed the role of language, of the Saussurian 'signifier' in any text, and have written in a way which has drawn attention to issues of language as central. Language may be used to maintain conventional thought: to serve, specifically, the interests of the bourgeoisie, or it may be so twisted, so used to 'defamiliarize', as the Russian Formalists demanded, that it baffles conventional opinion and the inert reception of ideas. The stress on the literary 'device' whereby the text turns the reader from conventional thought, becomes central. At the same time, Modernism is sceptical about the ability to pass from the word to a clear referent: to make the transition from language to the real world, from the 'signifier' to the 'signified', and this new sense

that there is only *writing*, merely the signifier, no signified, both
sanctions such radical suggestions as Mallarmé's that the poet 'cede
the initiative to words'[6] and invites the thought that the text gives
simply the play of the signifier, the play of writing. (I use 'play' in
both its ludic sense, and also in the way we speak of 'play' within the
component parts of a piece of machinery.)

The English Modernists and critics – Lawrence, Eliot, Pound,
Empson, Leavis – are quite out of sympathy with this relegation of
'meaning', broadly speaking: and the contrast is strong: English
criticism has not dealt with language as 'literary', because that would
allow for the notion of the play of text, rather than for the sense of
language bringing to light, or creating, 'reality'.

In the next chapter, we shall focus on Jakobson's work in more
detail.

4. Language Structures in Literature

... what he had in his studio were almost all seascapes done here at
Balbec. But I was able to discern from these that the charm of each of
them lay in a sort of metamorphosis of the objects represented,
analogous to what in poetry we call metaphor, and that, if God the
Father had created things by naming them, it was by taking away their
names or giving them other names that Elstir created them anew.
                                      Proust: *Within a Budding Grove*

The word 'literary' receives a new meaning from the Russian Formalists and Jakobson, who wrote that 'the subject of literary science is
not literature, but literariness, i.e. that which makes a given work a
literary work'. I have given the word an emphasis in order to stress
how new it is. Doctor Johnson's 'Literary Club' would not have

understood what this use of the adjective 'literary' meant: for Johnson, all writing would be, of necessity, literary, as we have already seen. But then, neither would Johnson have appreciated Jakobson's declaration that poetry is 'organized violence committed on ordinary speech'. For Jakobson, in contrast to Doctor Johnson, is working within a sense that within the structure of the *langue*, there must be a strong deviation towards the poetic or literary in an individual statement; while Doctor Johnson would never have thought in terms of poetry offering more than 'general truths' which came out of the *langue*, would never have thought that an individual statement should be sharply differentiated from the general order of statements. 'Gray thought his language more poetical as it was more remote from common use', he commented in his *Life of Gray*:[1] arguing strongly against eccentricity in the use of poetic language.

Jakobson believed that these poetic deviations could and should be examined from the perspective of linguistics, by the attempt to think scientifically about language. Formalism, and the Prague circle of linguistics, to which he belonged before the Second World War, stressed the *function* of any utterance, as a way of defining its nature. In 1958, in his 'Closing statement: Linguistics and poetics', Jakobson stressed six functions within any utterance. These functions are 'set towards' either the sender of the message, or to the receiver of it, or to the context of meaning in which the utterance exists, or to the actual message, or to the contact that exists between sender and receiver, or, finally, to the code that it is framed in. Taking these in order, we get:

1 *The emotive function*: this expresses the attitudes and feelings of the person speaking.
2 *The conative*: which relates to the way the message is intended to influence the receiver.
3 *The referential*: where the stress is on the content contained in the speech. The referential function refers to the context of the speech: to the outside world, in fact.
4 *The poetic*: this draws attention to the verbal structure of the message, emphasizes it, stresses its nature as an utterance.
5 *The phatic*: which makes and keeps contact between people. Discussion of the weather is often phatic: it serves no other function.
6 *The metalingual*. This works to explain the code in which an utterance is framed.

Jakobson argues that all these functions may work in an utterance: the question is whether any of them are dominant. As an exercise, try deciding which is the dominant function in each of the following sentences:

1 The rain in Spain stays mainly in the plain.
2 Call me Ishmael.
3 Friends, Romans, countrymen, lend me your ears.
4 Thirty years ago, Marseilles lay burning in the sun, one day.
5 I have a great deal of difficulty in beginning to write my portion of
   these pages, for I know I am not clever.
6 That was a way of putting it – not very satisfactory.

DISCUSSION

My answer runs: the first sentence is *poetic*, the second, *phatic*, the
third *conative*, the fourth, *referential*, the fifth, *emotive* and the sixth,
metalinguistic. At the same time, there was a twist to each, for they
are all 'literary' utterances, in the sense that they all come out of bits
of literature.

The first, from *My Fair Lady*, draws attention to itself by rhyme,
assonance, alliteration and by the sense that its referential content is
low. It only exists to provide the opportunity for play in staging: as
does the similar number from *Singin' in the Rain*, 'Moses supposes
his toes are roses / But Moses supposes erroneously'. The second,
which opens *Moby Dick*, establishes a jaunty contact, which makes
it difficult to know whether the name of the Biblical outcast Ishmael
is to be taken ironically or at face value. The third, from *Julius
Caesar*, is a line of poetry, and also rhetorical persuasion. Note its
rhythm: one syllable, two, three, up to the main caesura or pause:
then four monosyllables in contrast to that build up. I see it as
predominantly conative, but it is also referential, and phatic. The
fourth, which opens *Little Dorrit*, is clearly referential, yet poetic too
– note the antithesis between the two lengths of time at the beginning
and end of the sentence, and also the loaded metaphor of 'burning'.
More than that, it advertises itself as being within a code of narration
– 'Thirty years ago' is very like 'Once upon a time', and thus the
referential statement presents itself as a twist upon the 'fairy tale'
motif. Note, too, the assonances: Mars*eilles* – lay – day; and sun –
one. The fifth opens Esther Summerson's narrative in *Bleak House*,
and establishes her as a character, yet the neatness of the formulation
slyly contradicts her point that she is not clever: note the alliterations, for example. The last is from Eliot's *Four Quartets*, and
comments – as so much Modernist poetry does – on the frames
of reference used, on the style. Eliot criticizes his own work as
he goes along, and indeed, much literary criticism is effectively
metalinguistic.

*

It might be said that these six functions of language operate in all literary languages, then, but that Jakobson wishes to give special place to the poetic function of language where the statement 'thickens language, drawing attention to its formal properties' as he puts it in the 'Closing statement'. In other words, whether it is prose or verse, you can still find the poetic function, when the reader becomes strongly aware of the language, rather than of its sender, receiver, of its meaning, or of its code, or of the fact that it belongs to a contact. What do you think of this definition? How well does it apply to the poetry looked at – the 'Anecdote of the Jar' (p. 24) and the lines by Pope (p. 12)?

DISCUSSION

My provisional reaction is that it works as an account of some Modernist writing: but it is harder to apply it to, say, Pope's *Essay on Man*, which reads as versified philosophy, with little sense of a difference between the referential and the poetic uses of language, and where style is itself part of meaning, as we saw when we looked at the couplet from the *Essay on criticism*. (Yet it fits Duck's poem, written as it is in a very self-consciously 'literary' ('neo-classical') way.) Modernist writing separates form and content more consciously, and often – as in Joyce, or Mann, or Kafka – suggests that what is being written is actually only a way of writing: there is no truth content to the passage apart from that. But if each of the six quotations exhibits some literary features, because of where they come from – though they may not all be 'poetic' in the specialized sense that Jakobson is using the term – does it really get us much further to use his terminology?

In a paper called 'How ordinary is ordinary language?',[2] the American critic Stanley Fish criticizes Formalist (and specifically Jakobsonian) ideas of the 'poetic' use of language as something that deviates from the norm by saying that 'deviation theories trivialize the norm', and argues that 'there is no such thing as ordinary language'. He stresses that there is something rhetorical, persuasive, indeed, about all speech acts, and says that literature is 'language around which we have drawn a frame, a frame that indicates a decision to regard with a particular self-consciousness the resources language has always possessed'. In other words, literature is in the eye of the beholder, and Fish, whose reputation has been founded on his analysis of the way a reader decides to take a text ('reception theory' is the term for this), is suggesting that the 'frame' can only be artificially imposed.

It might be interesting to associate this view with Raymond Williams's much more politically engaged one, which notes the 'extraordinary ideological feat' that has made literature seem more particular and immediate than the 'actual lived experiences of society and history'[3] (*Marxism and literature* (Oxford, 1977) p. 46). In other words, to place 'creative literature' above ordinary language, to say that *this* is where 'life' is, makes ordinary language a poor relation, and denies people's spontaneity and creativity in language – or, to return to Fish their rhetorical skill in language. Leavis's sense of poetic uses of language coming out of the ordinary spoken language of the community will be recalled.

Williams suggests that nineteenth-century political interests 'drew a frame' around certain types of writing, so that they could become 'literature': we have explored some of the reasons for doing this in Chapter 1. Fish's argument is less politically acute than Williams's, in that the assumption that texts are constructed as literature in the way they happen to be read is perhaps true but only of academic interest in that literature exists as a massive historical institution, and the freedom to read in one way or another is actually limited, often by academic constraints. Jakobson could have fairly replied to Fish that it is no doubt true that there is no such thing as *ordinary* language; but that does not affect the issue that language cannot be thought of ahistorically, statically: its condition is that it is an activity, used competitively by different dominant interests. For new insights to emerge, for consciousness to emerge further, there has to be a deviation from the norm. Fish's position, in that respect, is too easy, too compliant with the 'norm'.

Jakobson on metaphor and metonymy

In the last chapter, Saussure's work in linguistics was mentioned as a crucial influence on Formalism, as also on the Prague circle. The individual speech act is derived from the *langue*, and the process of choice of words operates in a dual manner. Saussure contended that the process of choice of a word was dual; both *syntagmatic* and *associative*. In the first place, the word – say 'book' – has to be plucked from its syntactic and possible sequential relationships and use of it is governed by the sense of how it can function in a meaningful sequence of words. And the word 'book' summons up comparative associations – 'magazine', 'newspaper', – those words which suggest things the 'book' is not, and which play around it hauntingly. For Saussure, to think of a book is to think of it both in relationship to its use in a sentence, and in relationship to other types of reading material. In the second place, to think of the book is to think of its associations – red, black, good, for example, to give three possible adjectives. Thus we have:

1 An axis of language which may be thought of as a horizontal line. Here one word is associated with another, and a process of contiguity between one word and the next invites us to move on from one word to the next. This is the *syntagmatic* axis.

2 A *paradigmatic*, axis, which is vertical, where one word relates to another because their meanings and associations overlap, or substitute one for another.

Jakobson, in a famous piece of research published in 1956 as 'Two aspects of language and two types of aphasic disturbance'[4] made an important and controversial extension of Saussure's theory. He suggested that memory loss may be seen acting on the two axes of language. Thus aphasics, (people with a loss of speech due to a cerebral disturbance) who suffered a memory loss on the line of contiguity found either substitute words, or ones with an opposite meaning – 'hut' might produce 'cabin' or 'palace'. Those with the loss on the line of similarity, found words like 'burnt down' or 'poor little house' or 'thatch' or 'litter'. He associated the first type with metonymy, where one term replaces another, or stands in for it, as 'Downing Street' (as in a BBC report – 'Downing Street said tonight that it had no comment to make . . .') appears as a metonym for the Prime Minister, or where 'sail' is used instead of 'boat'. The word 'metonymy' literally means 'change of name'. Where the part of something is put for the whole, the figure is, precisely, *synecdoche*. The second type he associated with the use of metaphor, where the replacement word(s) enrich the missing term. Metaphor replaces one signifier by another that it might possibly evoke in an imaginative or in a logical way. To illustrate these distinctions, you may find it worthwhile to go back to the six sentences on p. 38 to identify examples of both metaphors and metonymy. Make a separate list of each where you think you find them.

DISCUSSION

Metaphor   I have already helped you with sentence 4. Marseilles is not really burning: that is an imaginative evocation that the narrator adds to the fact that Marseilles was in the sun: I suppose 'lay' is another metaphor, so that the city is compared to a body – perhaps a bit of meat cooking? In sentence 6, 'a way' is a metaphor so tired you may not have noticed it, but there is, just about, the idea of travelling in the word (and it is elsewhere in the poem). In 5, I suppose 'portion' is a metaphor: from the more neutral word 'part', imaginative associations develop, so that a 'portion' may have further associations (such as those of food?). If it takes some time to recognize these as metaphors, then it shows how literary language itself is only an intensification of ordinary language, which is already packed full of metaphorical devices – the *teeth* of a saw; the *spine* of a book for instance.

Metonymy The outstanding example is in 3 – 'Lend me your ears': where 'ears' displaces 'attention', or 'hearing' – what you do with your ears, – or 'minds' – what is on the other side of the ear, as it were. 'These pages' in 5 looks like metonymy for 'book'; similarly, 'rain' in 1 is metonymic for all forms of precipitation: snow and hail are included. In 2, 'Ishmael' might be metonymic: if you have to call the narrator something, then you move along the whole range of names that suggest different qualities, and there is the suggestion that quite a few of them would do, that 'Ishmael' is only one possibility. If you doubt that, compare how the novel could conceivably have opened – 'My name is Ishmael', and see where the difference is.

Jakobson's point is that language oscillates between these two axes of metaphor and metonymy, and that some forms of writing use primarily either one or other of them: Romantic poetry primarily uses metaphor, and the realist novel uses metonymy. The axis of contiguity has to do with syntactical arrangements, with a 'logical' sense of how words can be used each with each: and that order is strongly associated with the eighteenth- and nineteenth-century novel. In contrast, poetry works, crucially, through its ability to find surprising comparisons. It projects, as Jakobson says poetic language does, 'the paradigmatic and metaphoric dimension of language onto the syntagmatic'. In other words, the steadiness of that syntactic, associative code with its sense of narrative is disrupted. Can you see how that works with this first quatrain from Shakespeare's Sonnet 73? Where do metaphorical effects cut across, or disrupt narrative progress?

> That time of year thou may'st in me behold
> When yellow leaves, or none, or few, do hang
> Upon those boughs which shake against the cold;
> Bare ruined choirs, where late the sweet birds sang.

DISCUSSION

It begins as a quiet piece of communication: as though the speaker is speaking to someone. But already in the first line, metaphor has entered in: something in the persona is compared to the seasons: is it his age? His inspiration? His feeling of depression? The metaphor of autumn–winter takes over and begins a new narration, which is developed by the metaphor of the leaves and the boughs: this goes up to the end of the third line, but then the fourth caps that metaphor by using the metaphor of 'choirs'. Are these 'choirs' literal choirs of singers? In which case 'sweet birds' is a further metaphor for them; or are they metaphors for the avenue of trees that look faintly like Gothic pillars in a cathedral where the 'choirs' sang? But then you will be aware that part of a church building is called 'the choir', as a metonymy for the section of the edifice where the choristers sing. Thus one image – the trees, which is already metaphorical for the way it implies the age of the poet – suggests a further metaphor: the church, which leads to a metonymic association, of building with singers, who are metaphorically (by being called 'birds') linked back to the trees.

If that sounds puzzling, you might be further interested to know that in the original printing of the *Sonnets*, the word 'choirs' is actually 'quiers', which put into modern English directly, would turn out as 'quires' – sheaves of paper. Is the poet referring to his loss of inspiration? All he writes just ruins the paper? His poetry no longer sings? You could work out a possible new interpretation on these lines.

But what is the relationship between the fourth line and the others? It is certainly not a necessary one. The narrative flow of the first three lines, such as it is, is interrupted by this strangely imagistic line, which syntactically comes after the end of a sentence: it could simply have finished its sense with the word 'cold': the fourth line looks like a master-metaphor to fill out the others.

'Leaves' may imply the leaves of a tree, or the leaves of a book: Orlando, in *As You Like It* hung his 'leaves' of poetry on the boughs: perhaps the image in lines 2–3 is of fading inspiration: if he could hang his leaves, like Orlando, they would only be faded ones? (So that perhaps the memory of art, of singing, in the fourth line represents a personal nostalgia?) Do the leaves suggest the laurel crown, and if so, is the withered state an emblem of faded glory? Do 'boughs' in line 3 imply by their 'shaking' old and palsied limbs? Old people feel the cold more: is that the sense? And if so, is the presence of a human head felt in the word 'bare'? Was that what the absence of leaves was implying: the bald pate? Yet the bareness suggests, by the end of the line, the lately ruined (after 1533 – some sixty years before this was written) abbeys and monasteries, where both literal and metaphorical sweet birds sang.

Sonnet 73 thus might be said to fit Jakobson's definition, though the narrative is not disrupted, only filled out. Again, it might be argued that the kind of break-up of the line of contiguity that

Jakobson wants is characteristic of modernist poetry, where the need for 'defamiliarization' does involve a turning around of the ordinary, commonsense reality.

But Jakobson's position has been argued with.[5] It has been pointed out that he ignores entirely the sound value of the signifier: that his definition of the insertion of the metaphoric axis onto the metonymic is intended only at the level of meaning – at the level of the 'signified' as Saussure would say – and that part of the whole argument of Saussure is that signifiers connect on the paradigmatic relationship also on the level of sound value – thus book: look: cook are linked. The aural nature of the poetic is thus played down in Jakobson.

Nonetheless, that said, Jakobson's 'principle of equivalence' works well as an account of rhyme and assonance, where aural effects of identity (i.e. the rhymes) cut across semantic effects – that is, the meaning. (This is to link the aural effects with metaphor; the semantic ones with metonymy.) The effect is thus to disengage the words (the signifiers) from their habitual signifieds, and emphasize 'the palpability of the sign'. Take these examples – first from Dryden's *Absalom and Achitophel*:

> Great wits are sure to madness near allied,
> And thin partitions do their bounds divide.

Here the rhyme of allied/divide brings together two signifiers contrasted in meaning. The rhyme thus underwrites the meaning, that clever people are near to madness. Similarly, in these last lines from Hopkins's 'Spring and Fall: to a young child'

> It is the blight man was born for,
> It is Margaret you mourn for.

Here the rhyme associates birth and death (mourning) as one thing, whereas ordinary sense would keep them apart. The rhyme enforces another meaning, one which the poem's sense strives towards.

Other criticisms of Jakobson may be mentioned more briefly, and left for consideration. It has been objected to Jakobson that he conflates the syntagmatic with the idea of syntax too easily: thus the axis of contiguity becomes associated too quickly with the idea of realist writing, and with a 'commonsense' understanding of the world. And lastly, it is contended that his system blends the concepts of *langue* and *parole* too hastily: it is assumed that what happens in the movement from *langue* to *parole* is replicated straightforwardly in the movement from a person's way of talking – their grammar, indeed – into their poetic way of thinking.

However, the consideration of metaphor and metonymy does open up texts usefully. Consider the language of the following passage from *Mansfield Park* (1814), by Jane Austen (1775–1817), and examine its language uses. Is the passage rich metaphorically? Can you pick out examples of metonymy within it? Can you find connected passages within it that suggest the axis of contiguity? What other elements of poetic writing, or rhetorical devices do you find here? The passage opens the novel thus:

> About thirty years ago, Miss Maria Ward, of Huntingdon, with only seven thousand pounds, had the good luck to captivate Sir Thomas Bertram, of Mansfield Park, in the county of Northampton, and be thereby raised to the rank of a baronet's lady, with all the comforts and consequences of a handsome house and large income. All Huntingdon exclaimed on the greatness of the match, and her uncle, the lawyer, himself, allowed her to be at least three hundred pounds short of any equitable claim to it. She had two sisters to be benefited by her elevation; and such of their acquaintance as thought Miss Ward and Miss Frances quite as handsome as Miss Maria, did not scruple to predict their marrying with almost equal advantage. But there certainly are not so many men of large fortune in the world as there are pretty women to deserve them. Miss Ward, at the end of half a dozen years, found herself obliged to be attached to the Reverend Mr Norris, a friend of her brother in law, with hardly any private fortune . . . they began their career of conjugal felicity with very little less than a thousand a year.

DISCUSSION

1   Metaphor, 'Captivate' – to make captive, clearly: the image is derived not too distantly from the hunting-field: the word is half-way between what you would expect to be said about someone attractive, and a comment on a predatory nature. But this 'thickening of language' apart, there is not much metaphor here, though what about 'match', and 'career'?

2   'All Huntingdon' (once one of the smallest of counties) is a metonym: the phrase does not mean everyone in Huntingdon, or probably even half, but the few families that are involved, or that have read about the marriage in the papers. But, in a sense, the whole passage is constructed on metonyms, where something is said that conceals – or only hints at – something else: Maria has no qualities recorded apart from her money, and if she is three hundred pounds short of any claim, that seems to be all she is short of. No one looks any further: as it were, they think in metonymy. A similar point might be made about Mr Norris. Nor is anything said about Sir Thomas: a metonymy here allows him a 'handsome house and a

large income' only; and a transference appears to have taken place: the man should (traditionally) be handsome and the house large, and the income not mentioned by a process of polite metonymy where that is skipped over, but such writing displaces all these categories, and this seems to be the essence of metonymy. It also suggests that metonymy is a technique to make irony possible. Everyone associates Jane Austen with that quality, where one thing is said and something contiguous meant, and metonymy is just the device by which that can happen. But it seems interesting that the metonymy seems to work in reverse. Good manners should prevent you from being so unabashedly economic in your way of discussing: the narrator's voice omits all the conventional talk and has already decoded it, as it were, so that there is a strong sense that the narration is giving a commentary on the conventional utterances of middle-class society – showing what lies behind and beyond their polite statements.

Note, too, the 'transferred epithet' – 'handsome' is applied first to the house, then to the sisters. Clearly there is an association of ideas, and it seems to have a metonymic value, therefore: but what does it do to the meaning of the word in both cases?

3   My candidates for chains of associated ideas are first, the references to numbers that go through the passage: thirty: seven thousand: three hundred: two: half a dozen: a thousand. Is this predominance a reflection on the calculation that is so evident in the society depicted? Or do the references to numbers build up that reading of a mercenary society? Secondly, the phrasing which builds up a character description after each name: compare what is said after 'Miss Maria Ward', with what comes after 'Sir Thomas Bertram'; and 'the Reverend Mr Norris'. Is it a case of people being assessed simply by what comes after their names, and is that assessment made through an automatic process of detailing what things are conventionally associated with them? In this way, the whole narration proceeds on a straightforward pathway of contiguous relationships. We hear first about one sister, then the next (and then the last); and perhaps that code of logical development is being played on by Austen so that we gather that an order has been disrupted: the eldest sister (Miss Ward – the name indicates she is eldest) has not been married first, and this all suggests volumes in terms of jealousy, etc. which the rest of the book will pick up on. But only an understanding of this narrative, metonymic code will give the reader this point.

4   There is some self-consciously poetic language here. You will have picked up the alliterations – raised–rank; comforts–consequences; handsome house, for instance. Note the antithesis: 'many men of large fortune' . . . 'pretty women'; note, too, how (just like the

opening of *Little Dorrit*, though of course that is written later), Austen's start advertises the beginning of a tale; it engages a narrative code, indicating that we are plunging in, perhaps suggests that we are to expect much information to be given us. Lastly, recalling Bakhtin's sense of the plural voices to be heard in the novel, how many voices are there in the passage? My own count would be: perhaps the voice of the newspapers in the first sentence, the voice of polite Huntingdon and the lawyer in the second, the remarks of friends in the third, the voice of 'received opinion' in the fourth, and something, perhaps, of Miss Ward's private feelings in the fifth. There is also, of course, an elusive narrator's voice, which contains all these 'others' within it.

For a second example, take the opening of Virginia Woolf's *Mrs Dalloway*, (1925):

> Mrs Dalloway said she would buy the flowers herself.
>
> For Lucy had her work cut out for her. The doors would be taken off their hinges; Rumpelmayer's men were coming. And then, thought Clarissa Dalloway, what a morning – fresh, as if issued to children on a beach.
>
> What a lark! What a plunge! for so it had always seemed to her, when, with a little squeak of the hinges, which she could hear now, she had burst open the French windows and plunged at Bourton into the open air. How fresh, how calm, stiller than this of course, the air was in the early morning, like the flap of a wave, the kiss of a wave, chill and sharp . . .

Here, look at the patterns of this prose, and ask whether it associates predominantly metonymically or metaphorically.

DISCUSSION

The passage does work strongly through associations, not always clear on the surface. The cut flowers of the first line lead to the 'cut out' expression of the second, on a purely verbal and hidden pattern (and 'sharp' belongs here too), just as the removal of the doors suggests the opening of the windows (which Clarissa did at Bourton thirty-two years previously). Plunging into the fresh air (just as the flowers will be fresh) implies being on the beach, which then leads to associations of the sea, and presumably, running into the sea. (Those who know the novel will remember that one of its main actions involves a man throwing himself out of a window to his death on the railings below: this action seems strongly anticipated throughout the passage.) I think this patterning is metonymic in character.

But it is crossed with something else. Take the sentence beginning 'And then . . .'. What does 'then' refer to? In context, it ought to refer to the time after the doors are taken off their hinges. Actually, it is not a word which invokes time at all: it starts the second reason for Mrs Dalloway going out to buy flowers. A temporal clause is disrupted, and that disruption of linearity, of continuance in time, is characteristic of Woolf: in the next paragraph, after 'What a lark! What a plunge!' about which we cannot be sure in what time it belongs, present or past, the narrative recalls the past at Bourton as something that can be lived again. The imagery of the wave, in a repeated phrase gives a metonymic association – from 'flap' to 'kiss' (and nothing more metonymic than one wave succeeding another), yet the very comparison of the air to the water is metaphoric, disrupting again a clear linear flow.

Thus while the dominant mode here is metonymic, with the progress of time and regular association of ideas suggesting the realist novel form, there is a poetic – metaphoric – intrusion onto this syntagmatic progression. Thematically, the attempt to undercut the metonymic line is important in that the novel is trying to break up the dominance of linear time, perceived to be a monotonous oppression. The novel tries to 'thicken' time, as it were, in each of its moments and to evade the sense of its sequentiality implying loss. And that idea is generated from the metaphoric axis of language intruding onto the metonymic, that which stands for commonsensical, indifferent, and for Virginia Woolf, dominating patriarchal order, which itself represses, and which she writes against.

The result of this examination may well suggest that there is justice in Jakobson's sense of two axes of language: the metonymic being more applicable to the realist novel and the metaphoric to poetry. At any rate, there are important working suggestions to be taken from the idea that the writer proceeds along the code of associative connections, and can disrupt them at will from that other axis.

The Pursuit of Structure

Jakobson developed further the sense of the poetic, which he tended more and more to identify with poetry itself, in a paper called 'poetry of grammar and grammar of poetry' (1968) where he decided 'one might say that in poetry similarity is superimposed on contiguity, and hence "equivalence is promoted to the constitutive device of the sequence"'. Two years later, with Lawrence Jones, he produced an analysis of Shakespeare's sonnet 129 which was designed to demonstrate this point. I quote the poem from Stephen Booth's scholarly edition.[6] Before continuing with Jakobson's account, look at it in terms of its structure. If the poem is not familiar to you, you will need to spend some time looking at it. Observe its symmetries, where one part echoes another, its parallelisms of language or of similar formations of phrases – and even symmetries in groups of letters. Its formal structure is evident: three quatrains (four lines each, rhymed ABAB) followed by a rhymed couplet.

> Th'expense of spirit in a waste of shame
> Is lust in action, and till action, lust
> Is perjured, murd'rous, bloody, full of blame,
> Savage, extreme, rude, cruel, not to trust,
> Enjoyed no sooner but despisèd straight,
> Past reason hunted, and no sooner had
> Past reason hated, as a swallowed bait
> On purpose laid to make the taker mad;
> Mad in pursuit and in possession so,
> Had, having, and in quest to have, extreme,
> A bliss in proof, and proved, a very woe,
> Before, a joy proposed, behind, a dream.
> > All this the world well knows, yet none knows well
> > To shun the heav'n that leads men to this hell.

DISCUSSION

There are striking parallelisms here which Jakobson pointed out, and reversals, too: 'Is lust in action' / 'action lust Is'; 'mad/Mad' (lines 8–9), 'well knows' / 'knows well', 'All this' / 'this hell'. This kind of word reversal is called a *chiasmus*. There are conjunctions, too, like the assonance of 'hated', 'bait', 'laid', 'make', 'taker', 'mad', 'mad', 'had'. Then, too, 'purpose' ... 'pursuit', and then the *metathesis* (exchange of letters) to 'proof', 'proved' and 'proposed'. The last word, in a different part of speech (verb, not noun) is etymologically and historically the same as the first in the group, 'purpose'. Combinations of letters that seem interesting are, for example, *exp*ense, *sp*irit, wa*st*e, lu*st*, *ext*reme, tru*st*, de*sp*ised, pa*st*, and so on. You have probably found other examples, of alliteration, combinations of letters and contrasts. Many of these are not easy to work out. For instance, note 'before' and 'behind', as a verbal contrast in line 12. The commas Booth gives are not in the original 1609 Quarto, and since 'proposed' comes from a Latin root meaning 'to place in front of', 'before' and 'behind' could refer to either time or place. Thus the line could suggest either, 'Before the lust is consummated, it seems joyful, but afterwards it exists as something without substance, empty', or 'it seems like a joy set forth to someone under cover of a dream, i.e. a fantasy'. These differences of sense are strong, and suggest the open nature of the writing.

Jakobson works out an elaborate series of equivalences between the first seven lines and the last seven, between the first and third verses (*strophes*) and the second and last, between the two outer ones and the two inner ones, and the two 'central' lines, 'Past reason hunted . . . taker mad', where he finds the only simile, and so the only comparative construction, 'as . . .'. All these contrasts and equivalences he calls 'binary oppositions'; the whole poem being constructed on them; on the principle that one idea is set in sharp contrast to another. (It might be relevant to add that Jakobson was working under the influence of Lévi-Strauss' structuralist approach.)

To speak thus about equivalences and contrasts (which, of course, suggest equivalences in reverse) may well suggest that the sonnet works simply by its piling up of similarities/dissimilarities – which suggests the metaphorical axis – onto the axis of contiguity, where a statement is being made. And Jakobson is certainly convincing in suggesting the subtleties there are at the level of structure. At the level he has identified, Shakespeare is certainly 'poetic', according to his terminology. But are there any reservations to be made about the approach?

One first point you might notice is that this dealing with structure says little about meaning. It is no criticism of Jakobson to complain that his account of the Sonnet actually says little about anything referential in it: but it does comment on the bearing of linguistic structures on meaning. Actually, I think Jakobson misreads at one point. He sees a similar grammatical construction in the middle lines quoted and in the final couplet and argues that the villain is heaven which destroys men. Note, in this connection, the similarity between the words 'laid' and 'leads'. Now this is a radical reading, but it seems to me to leave out the way that the second quatrain is going. From line 5 on, the words 'enjoyed', 'had', 'hated', 'laid' seem strongly suggestive of sexual intercourse and of an attitude to the woman who is certainly involved – any edition of the poem will explain at length the puns on the specifically male sexuality in the first line – but which is metonymically displaced, spoken about as 'lust'. The sense of who makes the taker mad is that, if any agency is involved, it is the woman. I am not saying that this is a necessary reading, but it seems to me to exclude Jakobson's. In other words, analysis of structure by itself cannot replace attention to referentiality.

The second point is made by an American critic, Michael Riffaterre, whose work complements Jakobson's, and is interesting in its own right. He takes Jakobson's analysis of a Baudelaire poem, 'Les chats', and asks, 'Can we not suppose . . . that the poem may contain certain structures that play no part in its function and effect as a literary work of art, and that there may be no way for structural linguistics to distinguish between these unmarked structures and those that are inherently active? Conversely, there may well be strictly poetic structures that cannot be recognized as such by an analysis not geared to the specificity of poetic language'. Later he comments on one structure that it 'makes use of constituents that cannot possibly be perceived by the reader; these constituents must therefore remain alien to the poetic structure, which is supposed to emphasise the form of the message, to make it more "visible", more compelling'.[7]

Riffaterre's critique comes from someone expert in nineteenth-century French poetry, where there is, in the later part of the century, precisely an interest in the form of the poem, and the sense that it has inner cohesion, and little referentiality – Mallarmé comes to mind straightaway. So it is not surprising that Riffaterre's *The Semiotics of Poetry* should deal precisely with what 'the poem' does, as though this were a kind of absolute. Riffaterre borrows from Jakobson when he suggests that 'literature, by saying something, says something else' (p. 17);[7] and argues that in reading poetry, there is more awareness of the way things are said, rather than of what is said.

The first reading of a poem, which he calls 'heuristic' – exploratory, making discoveries – is followed, he says, by a sense of its *ungrammaticality*, its threatening of traditional literary mimesis. 'Mimesis' means 'imitation' – the representation of reality. So, in other words, Riffaterre is saying that we first read a poem as though it represents, or refers to the world outside us, and then we do a double-take on that reading to see that the poem doesn't cohere, doesn't quite work at the level. The reader has to learn to see how the text is actually deforming that existing sense of reality, and has to take the text in a second way, hermeneutically. Here the poem 'twists the mimetic codes out of shape by substituting its own structure for their structures' (p. 13). As Riffaterre lists the ways poems vary stylistically from a normal pattern, he sounds a little like Empson enumerating different types of ambiguity, but the crucial point he argues is that the actual meaning of the poem is very slight: it reduces, actually, to a simple straightforward word or sentence which he calls a matrix. (But its origin is not the matrix: it is much more complex than that.) The poem then is a series of tropes, or figures, or devices, playing on that matrix, putting the point again and again, in true metonymic fashion. The actual matrix never appears. There is, then, an abstract structure, in that sense comparable to Saussure's *langue*, from which the poem enacts its variations, as its own *parole*. Is there a matrix underpinning Sonnet 129? Can you suggest what it might be?

DISCUSSION

Booth in his edition of the *Sonnets* lists a number of then current proverbs that sum up, like a matrix, the content of Sonnet 129, such as 'Short pleasure, long lament', 'Hot love is soon cold', 'Love is lawless'. In Riffaterre's terms, any of these might be the matrix from which the poem works, and each of the quatrains and the couplet would be consistently developing it. The poem is no more than a series of variations on the unseen matrix, its distinguishing feature being the breakdown of orderly quatrains into one rush, as though under the influence of emotions. In the first quatrain, there are two definitions of lust – one of it in action, one before action. In the second quatrain, the condition of lust afterwards is depicted, and in the third, as Jakobson suggests, the emphasis turns onto the person who lusts, as does the final couplet. Meaning is thus limited: by the end, the paradigmatic sentence of the matrix has been exhausted.

Does this seem to limit the Sonnet? Riffaterre, following Bakhtin and Julia Kristeva, dwells on the poetic text being made up of a tissue of earlier ones: sayings in use and out of use, literary devices. *Intertextuality* is the name given to this sense that a text is woven by earlier forms of language: the word 'text', as we said in Chapter 2, etymologically implies a weaving. As Julia Kristeva puts it in *Desire in Language*, 'each word (text) is an intersection of words (texts) where at least one other word (text) can be read . . . any text is constructed as a mosaic of quotations; any text is the absorption and transformation of another'.[8]

What the poem does, according to Riffaterre, is generate a *significance* which is independent of its meaning, and which comes about from its reaccentuation of existing terms (he calls these 'hypograms'). So the poem comments on the discourse that produces it, on the 'ordinary language' – perhaps clichés, proverbs – which it stylistically deforms. Sonnet 129 is not a new poem about lust, on this reading, or an expression of the poet's point of view, perhaps discovered through his personal experience, as a Romantic interpretation would insist; but is instead a commentary on ways that lust, as something to be talked about, is enshrined in discourse. The sense of intensity generated in the poetic structure is a deliberate way of foregrounding the common trope that lust breaks all restraint, and generates, in the remorse that follows, a set of wild and whirling words. Riffaterre would stay much more with the idea of the poem as 'pure artifice' (p. 164) rather than conveying deep personal meaning.

Where Riffaterre differs from the New Critics and the whole English tradition of criticism is just in this attitude to meaning. I take it that he is implying that the poem converts and transforms those meanings and accepted senses that we take for granted and live by, to a certain extent. In that way, the poem has the power to deform, even subvert traditional meanings, traditional ways of representing ideas to one-self – traditional mimesis, in fact.

Formalism, and the emphasis on 'deviation' in Jakobson, stressed the distinctive marks of a poem, as an individual *parole* getting away from the *langue*. Something of that is still in Riffaterre, but with a difference. He refutes the category of ordinary language: he implies that all norms of speech are already 'intertexts': literary fragments, 'hot with intensified connotations, overloaded discourse', as he says, (p. 164). Ordinary speech, the hypograms that the poem works from, is not ordinary at all. We are made to think in literary terms, however conventionally we think. The poem has to escape from that prison of the overloaded system. Riffaterre goes beyond the Formalists in his much more theorized sense of the difficulty involved in saying that a text 'means' something: since whatever we wish to say has been said before, all literary language can do is further deviate from that overplus of 'meaning' and thus raise new possibilities of 'significance' in the mind of the reader.

Summary

We have traced through in these last two chapters, Jakobson's contribution to a study of the *structure* of literary texts. The Russian Formalists and Czech structuralists gave Jakobson the impetus to look at poetics in terms of linguistic figures ('tropes'): those of *metaphor* and *metonymy* being regarded as foundational. These two include within them earlier divisions of figures of thought; for example, sixteenth century writers on grammar and rhetoric, following Peter Ramus (1515–72), the French humanist, had thought of *synecdoche* (as in the use of 'sail' to describe a ship, or 'hands' to stand in for 'men'), and *irony* as dominant alongside metaphor and metonymy. Synecdoche perhaps may be included within the field of metaphor, and irony (where the meaning intended is contrary to that expressed) may be seen, as in our discussion of *Mansfield Park*, to belong with metonymy. In all, then, the twin master-concepts of metaphor and metonymy are fundamental for an understanding of how language operates, and Jakobson concentrates on how the poetic use of language must build up from them. Riffaterre argues, in contrast, that this attention to structure leaves out particular ways in which texts mean, rather than function structurally.

We will return to the fundamentals of figures of speech in the next chapter. In the meantime, it is enough to be aware of the metaphor/metonymy distinction, in order that this may be mapped onto a further sense of the rhetorical nature of all language, to which we will now turn.

5. Language, Rhetoric, Meaning

To take a famous example, there is no pun, double syntax, or dubiety of feeling in

> Bare ruined choirs, where late the sweet birds sang

but the comparison holds for many reasons . . . these, and many more relating the simile to its place in the Sonnet, must all combine to give the line its beauty, and there is a sort of ambiguity in not knowing which of them to hold most clearly in mind. Clearly this is involved in all such richness and heightening of effect, and the machinations of ambiguity are among the very roots of poetry.

William Empson: *Seven Types of Ambiguity*

We mentioned earlier Saussure's contrast of the *langue* and the *parole* of language, and his suggestion that linguists should study the first of these. His distinction between the 'signifier' and the 'signified' has also been touched on: he conceived a word as a sound image, the signifier, and a mental concept derived therefrom (the signified), and insisted that the link between these two is always wholly arbitrary. There is no reason why any signifier should summon up a particular signified: the relationship is never grounded on anything firm; even onomatopoeic signifiers of dogs barking, like 'bow-wow' are only conventional: in French, dogs are represented as barking differently, 'huah-huah', and in German 'wauwau'. For Saussure, meaning is only possible because signifiers exist in a whole chain, and one term in the chain exists differentially from another. Meaning arises because one signifier is not the same as the one next to it in the aural chain: 'rum' is different from 'rut' because of the 'm' and the 't'.

Indeed, language is defined as 'a system of differences without positive terms'.[1]

One signifier, therefore, comes to have meaning through conventional agreement; nonetheless language is a system of signs which can be wholly reaccentuated: alter the normal meaning of one, and everything changes in some degree. There is nothing outside language that keeps meaning in place, finally, though in practice a set of non-linguistic assumptions and patterns of living within different cultures fix meaning: otherwise language would be unusable. But still language is in a sense empty, comprising only material signifiers.

The point is important for its disagreement with Leavis' position. He demands that words enact meanings, as he says, discussing Hopkins, 'his use of words is not a matter of *saying* things with them; he is preoccupied with what seems to him the poetic use of them, and that is a matter of making them do and be'.[2] Any criticism which begins with the notion of the 'arbitrariness of the signifier' is going to make problems here. I am going to return to the philosophical divide towards the end of the next chapter, but here and for much of the next, I am going to pursue Saussure's direction, and its implications for 'literary language'.

Saussure's work was registered in Formalism, as we have seen, though its most popular influences have been felt in structuralist and post-structuralist thought. As part of a moment that both saw and made language as a distinct problem, it belonged to the Modernist movement: to that series of heterogeneous drives to grapple with the issue as to whether it is possible to break out of 'the prison house of language' to any definite, objective statement about the world, to any assertion that was referential in an unproblematic sense, to any use of language that was non-figurative, not turned back on itself. For Nietzsche (1844–1900), a proto-Modernist, it was not. Consider what he is saying here about language, and see, too, what it takes you back to from the last chapter.

> What then, is truth? A mobile army of metaphors, metonyms and anthropomorphisms – in short a sum of human relations, which have been enhanced, transposed, and embellished poetically and rhetorically, and which after long use seem firm, canonical and obligatory to a people: truths are illusions about which one has forgotten that this is what they are; metaphors which are worn out and without sensuous power.   'On truth and lie in an extra-moral sense' (1873)

It seems that Nietzsche holds, effectively, that all language is literary language. The gap between language that is referential, that reports objectively scientific truth, and poetic or imaginative writing is non-existent: even objective referential statements turn out to be metaphorical or metonymic. For all language, simply because it is in itself inherently empty – a conclusion Nietzsche arrived at before Saussure – has to be filled out, by the use of persuasive language, which, in other circumstances, we would certainly call 'literary'.

More, he is saying that all language is metaphor. We can understand that in two ways. The word 'book' stands in for the object it refers to: I do not, like the Laputans in Book 3 of *Gulliver's Travels*, carry around the object if I wish to refer to it in conversation: trouble is saved by using the word instead. But the word 'book' is not the object, book: and understanding rests on the listener's ability to know the difference. In that sense, the signifier 'book' has a metaphorical function, (it stands in place of something), and its associations do not fully comprehend what the object it describes is: the object is more than a 'book': it could be described differently. The implications are not serious in the case of the word 'book', perhaps: but what happens when I use the term 'God'? What does that refer to? For some people, it would refer to nothing at all. Here is language without an original reference-point, perhaps.

That point is older than Nietzsche, of course. His implication that all language is metaphor goes much further: it means that all statements are actually rhetorical, acts of persuasion. The British twentieth-century philosopher J. L. Austin distinguished between *constative* statements, where something is said that can be categorized as true/false, and *performative* statements, (such as 'I promise') where there is no proposition being made about the outside world – nothing 'referential', to use Jakobson. Whatever the force of 'I promise' – whether it does something to me, or to the person who hears me bind myself, no truth has been given. So for Austin, statements are either truth-telling, or persuasive.

Nietzsche would collapse that distinction. Here and elsewhere he is saying that even a referential statement is a rhetorical device, designed to persuade. Even the most basic logical axioms are not so much unchanging forms of thought, but express our inability, or disinclination, to think without these axioms. 'Ordinary' language is full of persuasive, performative statements, where the most basic proposition is an invitation to speaker or hearer to start, or to continue, to think in a certain way. Basic forms of sentence structure collude in this. When Nietzsche says in *Twilight of the Idols* (1888) 'I fear we are not getting rid of God because we still believe in grammar',[3] he implies that the common form of sentence in European languages, subject and predicate, imposes a way of thinking upon the user of sentences. The simple sentence 'The cat sat on the mat' gives a doer, the subject (the cat) and an object (the mat which got sat on). 'Sat on the mat' is the predicate (i.e. it gives what is said of the cat) in the example. Sentences then assume, by this distinction, a doer and an action. So in the sentence 'It's raining', we have both subject and predicate: 'It' (subject) 'is raining' (verb and predicate). But what is the 'it' that rains? It will not be hard here to see that 'it' refers to nothing at all, but you could argue, I suppose, that it encourages a belief that rain is caused by some mysterious force, God, or Nature, or suchlike . . . At any rate, the 'it' is metaphorical thought, and the subject–predicate form of sentences encourages a belief in causation: that all things have an agency activating them. Hence the remark about our belief in God.

Thus we return to the issue raised implicitly in Chapter 2 – that statements made about the 'real' world ultimately say more about the structure of language in use, give more illumination on the nature of the *langue* than about the nature of reality. Rather than people thinking and then using language (as Pope and the eighteenth century considered happened, so that poetry added style to previous thought), language uses people: gives them the illusion that they are thinking independently, whereas they are caught within the structure of the *langue*.

The use in Nietzsche of metaphor and metonymy will have reminded you of Jakobson's two axes of language, discussed in the last chapter. To combine the two positions is to decide that any statement about truth immediately swings away into a different statement altogether (metaphor), or subtly displaces the statement meant (metonymy). It is important now to supplement that account.

Psychoanalysis and Metaphor and Metonymy

The year Nietzsche died, Freud published his *Interpretation of Dreams* (1900), where, in Chapter 6, he employed the terms 'displacement' and 'condensation' to describe what happens when statements or ideas come to be represented in speech. It was a radical rethinking about the impossibility of a pure truth emerging in language: as radical as Saussure's, Freud's contemporary. To get at the point, it is necessary to think a little about how Freud conceived dreams. Briefly, in analysing the dream in order to get at its latent content by a process of interpretation, Freud held that there was a process of 'dream-work' which had to be transformed, the latent into the manifest content, which the dreamer reported. The dream-work censors and represses in a double process of 'condensation' and 'displacement', as well as by a 'secondary process' of revision that tries to pull the elements of the dream together into some order. Thus to read a dream, the analyst needs to see that each part of it has suffered a change. An element in the dream, such as a person who plays a crucial role in it, may actually be a condensation, may represent several people in real life: the image of the person is thus 'overdetermined' – i.e. produced from more than one source. Similarly, each element in the dream is actually a displacement of what the person feels: the censoring activity in the mind blots out one figure, or action, or word, replacing it with another.

The French psychoanalyst Jacques Lacan (1900–81) used the *Interpretation of Dreams* as his central text of Freud, and stressed that Freud had argued that the dream had a linguistic basis: to interpret the dream was to return to a group of words that fitted together in the dream like a rebus, a picture-puzzle. Lacan drew on Jakobson in his sense that condensation could be seen as a form of metaphor, and displacement as a form of metonymy. In an essay called 'The agency of the letter in the unconscious: or reason since Freud', (1957),[4] he set out the view that the child's entry into language, which he called the symbolic order, and associated with the rule of the Father, is radically disturbing, in that it condemns the user of language to an endless 'sliding of the signifiers' that make up language: to a constant condensation and displacement, of which metaphor and metonymy are good examples. He gives as an illustration of the two 'tropes' of metaphor and metonymy, a line out of Victor Hugo's poem 'Boaz endormi' ('Boaz asleep') (1859), on the Biblical patriarch Boaz, a rich and generous farmer, and the husband of Ruth, so an ancestor of Christ. Look at the line below, which gives two halves of a sentence which do not fit (in what sense is a 'sheaf' not miserly, but generous?). Do the categories of metaphor and metonymy help? (It may at this point be worth saying that Lacan took the example from a French dictionary of quotations designed to illustrate metaphor.)

> Sa gerbe n'était pas avare ni haineuse
> (His sheaf was neither miserly nor spiteful)

DISCUSSION

Lacan argues that 'His sheaf' is a metaphor – the signifiers here replace 'Boaz', who is neither miserly nor spiteful; and there is a further metaphoric association between the idea of generosity, which is a human quality, and implied here in the *human* terms used, and the fertility of the field, which is symbolized in the sheaf of corn. Furthermore, the axis of similarity works in terms of the sound of the signifiers, for Lacan says that 'gerbe' evokes 'verge' (a rod), which suggests the phallus; thus male power (patriarchy indeed), and the word 'gerbe' in any case means 'shower' or 'spray', which also implies the sexual fertility of the patriarch. These things are all condensed together: the choice of the word for 'sheaf' turns out to be overdetermined.

At the same time, did you think that 'gerbe' was metonymic? He is giving the sheaf to Ruth, so that the qualities in him are transferred, displaced, onto the sheaf, and the sheaf itself is a metonymy for all that Boaz has: his lands, his harvest. Moreover, if you wished to emphasize the sexual implication, there might certainly be a displacement of terms here. This only stresses that the two terms, metaphor and metonymy may be seen as alternative types of replacing and of slipping of language, and that Lacan has taken no more from Jakobson than the two possibilities of the sliding of the signifier than the names of the tropes. (Lacan would argue that the use of this line to illustrate metaphor in schools turns out not to be accidental: language enforces in every incidental the rule of patriarchy, of the dominant father.)

For a comparable English example, take this passage from Shakespeare, describing the death of Antony in *Antony and Cleopatra* IV.xv.64–8:

> O, wither'd is the garland of the war
> The soldier's pole is fall'n: young boys and girls
> Are level now with men: the odds is gone
> And there is nothing left remarkable
> Beneath the visiting moon.

'Pole' as metaphor for Antony, and his death (his 'fall') compresses ideas of the pole-star, the maypole, the banner. As it evokes power, it suggests certainly the phallus, which 'young boys and girls' lacking, as Lacan argues they perceive they do, within the rule of patriarchy, is the source of their perception of loss, and the reason for their easy insertion into the symbolic order. (Power is always elsewhere: actually no one according to Lacan, male or female, possesses the phallus.) The sexual sense of 'pole' is overdetermined by the accretion of other associations. Note the metonymic progressions: fall'n: level; the soldier's pole: the odds. Note how the intuition is repeated, with one formulation acting as metaphor for a previous metaphor, in the four-fold way of saying that there are no more men:

(a) the pole is fallen,
(b) young boys and girls are now equivalent to men,
(c) the odds is gone,
(d) nothing is left below the moon – a traditional image for the female.

Lacan would see the loss of the 'mark' (in the word 'remarkable') as significant in that it declares now the existence of a world of no positive terms. (The definition of language by Saussure offered at the beginning of the chapter, p. 54 should be recalled.) The phallus, valorized in patriarchal society, should be the privileged 'mark', which creates meaning and distinction, but it does not exist. The passage does not just mourn Antony, but turns his death into a metaphor for the loss of any privileged signifier: any signifier that could give ultimate meaning to language, keep it from turning into endless metaphor and metonymy.

What are the implications of Lacan's findings? They complete Jakobson's work in a radical way: by suggesting that rhetorical tropes actually correspond to something psychic: or, rather, that the unconscious, which, for Lacan, is 'structured like a language', can only work by using tropes that we associate with 'literary language'. That statement is rather packed, so let us consider it more fully.

Alongside Freud, who emphasized that the unconscious manifests itself in language – in jokes, slips of the tongue, in dreams, where the dream-content has a linguistic basis, Lacan draws on Saussure. For Saussure, you will recall, each 'signifier' means something only by its relationship to the next signifier within the whole chain that makes up the *langue*. Thus meaning is already dual: a statement cannot mean one thing *only*: it not only contains within it the sliding off into the signifiers that surround it: it entails the point that to say one thing is, at the same time, to be aware that its opposite has been excluded. The other, excluded term is still there, as an 'absence', as a 'trace' within the preferred term. Statements turn out to be double: the opposite is contained within the statement, however unitary it tries to be. (The affiliations of this position with Bakhtin's should be clear.)

For a first example, look at how ambiguity works in Polly Peachum's song to her parents, in John Gay's *The Beggar's Opera* (1728). She is asking that her highwayman husband should not be betrayed by them and hanged:

> For on the rope that hangs my dear
> Depends poor Polly's life.

Here the point to note is the meaning of 'depends', which means, literally, 'hangs from'. In saying that she will die if her husband is hanged, she (a) equates herself with her husband: he is, metaphorically, 'poor Polly's life'; (b) she implies that she is a weight on him, (c) more cynically, she suggests that poor Polly cannot live (i.e. enjoy

herself) unless her husband is hanged – a point her parents have been
trying to make to her. That third meaning is doubtless unconscious,
but once out, it cannot be got away from, especially when it fits so
neatly into the whole ideology of the text.[5]

There, ambiguity 'thickens' language, as Jakobson would say –
and you will notice Empson's point, quoted in the epigraph, that
ambiguity, doubleness, is basic to poetry, and so to literary language.
Another straightforward example of it occurs in the opening of
Keats's *Ode to Melancholy*:

> No, no; go not to Lethe, neither twist
> Wolf's-bane, tight-rooted, for its poisonous wine

On this, Empson commented that: 'somebody, or some force in the
poet's mind must have wanted to go to Lethe very much if it took
four negatives in the first line to stop them'.[6] Keats is rejecting suicide
then, yet, at the same time, entertaining it in his thoughts.

For a further example, Empson takes Hopkins's praise of a bird
in *The Windhover*, and especially the lines

> Brute beauty and valour and act, oh, air, pride, plume, here
> Buckle!

He reads 'buckle' to mean both 'to come together' (as in buckling a
belt) or 'to collapse' (as with a bicycle wheel). Read one way, the
implication is that there is a union of powerfully evoked physical
graces in Christ, or the windhover (which may be a metaphor for
Christ). Read another way, it may refer to the sufferings of Christ,
implying that all those vibrant qualities collapsed in him at his death,
which is, of course, permissible as a reading of a poem written by a
devout Jesuit. But it could also mean the breakdown of Hopkins's
spiritual life. The question is where the 'here' refers to: here, in the
whole flight of the bird (which may also be Christ), or here, in me. If
this reading works, Hopkins's life crashes round him in ruins.
Empson asks, 'What would Hopkins have said if he could have been
shown this analysis? . . . He would have denied with anger that he
meant "like a bicycle wheel", and then after much conscientious self-
torture would have suppressed the whole poem' (p. 226). That this
reading is not wayward seems to me evident from Hopkins's later
sonnets, with their near-despair – 'All / Life death doth end, and each
day dies with sleep' ('No worst, there is none'.)

The problem surfaces in questions of textual editing. Wilfred
Owen's 'Exposure', the first line of which I quoted in Chapter 2, ends
in most reprints of the poem thus:

> To-night, this frost will fasten on this mud and us,
> Shrivelling many hands, puckering foreheads crisp.
> The burying-party, picks and shovels in their shaking grasp,
> Pause over half-known faces. All their eyes are ice,
>   But nothing happens.

Leaving you at your leisure to pause over the assonance of 'eyes/ice', and the self-conscious richness of the language, I pass on to make the point that what Owen seems to have written is either 'To-night, this frost' or 'To-night, His frost'.[7] Put one way, the sense is neutral, put another way, in a poem which speaks about God in the previous stanza (it will be recalled that Owen considered himself a Christian), it sounds plaintive, almost attacking God. (The whole poem, which contains references to God, on whose account the soldiers lie out on the battlefield, is worth examining in this light.) I cannot see that an editor can opt for just one reading. The text seems to invite both possibilities – almost as though the neutral 'this' concealed a more dangerous – repressed – statement within it. An 'exposure' in a sense unintended by Owen is manifest: God is not on their side; the frost is part of the army against them; these thoughts cannot be kept out, but return, even with a slip of the pen.

This implies again duality in utterance: it is familiar in Shakespeare, and an actor saying the lines may have to make definite choices about how a speech is going to be understood (which suggests that 'literary language' exists both on the page and, sometimes, in a different way, in public reading or performance. Indeed, performance reminds us how labile texts are, how improvisatory, how unfixed.)

Thus an opposite sense haunts any existing signification. For Lacan, this is the unconscious, the Other, and it surfaces in the form of metaphor and metonymy, throwing up deviations which imply the absence of a central unitary truth. Insertion into language, for Lacan, means that the 'I' that speaks is dispersed among a chain of signifiers, where I cannot say anything unambiguously: all that I say is a temporary attempt to grasp at something, and all the time, the statement I make is haunted by the sense of the other, the repressed statement. Lacan formulates this sense of division, of doubleness by saying, 'It is not a matter of knowing whether I speak of myself in a way which conforms to what I am, but rather of knowing whether I am the same as that of which I speak'.[8] And the unconscious shows itself by those 'other' signifiers: it is, indeed, structured like a language.

The difficulty inherent in Lacan and Nietzsche is that it sounds as though it is impossible to say anything unambiguously: it makes conversation almost absurd in theory. There is no way round this save to say that Jakobson sees the referential use of language strongly bound by context: as was said in Chapter 3, most of our day-to-day speech has a strong boundary fixed on it by situation, repetition, the possibility of anticipation of what the other person wishes to say or is about to say, to say nothing of other signs we give – frowns, smiles, pointing with the finger. Speech takes place in a whole situation, so that it is not the only clue to meaning. As Dolly and her mother agree in *Anna Karenina* (VI.2), sexual attraction to another only needs 'looks and smiles' for its communication. When we talk in conceptual terms, however, problems arise; the total situation no longer helps, and misunderstanding is thoroughly possible. That said, however, the position of the Coleridgean critics who insist on looking at the actual poem on the page, not regarding the poem as a tissue of metaphors and metonymies centred around some meaning that is absent, is much to be sympathized with. The other position – the one outlined in this chapter – looks evasive, as though it were trying to avoid a confrontation with an actual meaning.

Nonetheless, the doubleness within language will surface: and especially in its poetic uses. Take this poem of George Herbert, (1593–1632), the Anglican priest and poet. His work characteristically thematizes the need to find an honest language to praise God in. The title, *Jordan (1)* suggests the need to rinse himself from impure statements, and the idea of baptism, and of the leper Naaman's washing in the River Jordan and thereby cleansing himself (2 *Kings* Ch. 5) are both relevant. The poem might be roughly paraphrased as 'You don't need to be rhetorical in order to write in praise of God: and I don't intend giving way to rhetoric'. In what ways, however, does the poem not say that, but the reverse?

> Who says that fictions only and false hair
> Become a verse? Is there in truth no beauty?
> Is all good structure in a winding stair?
> May no lines pass, except they do their duty
>   Not to a true, but painted chair?
>
> Is it no verse, except enchanted groves
> And sudden arbours shadow coarse-spun lines?
> Must purling streams refresh a lover's loves?
> Must all be veiled, while he that reads, divines,
>   Catching the sense at two removes?
>
> Shepherds are honest people; let them sing:
> Riddle, who list, for me, and pull for Prime:
> I envy no man's nightingale or spring;
> Nor let them punish me with loss of rhyme
>   Who plainly say, *My God, My King.*

DISCUSSION

I think I would answer the question by saying that the poem is absolutely rhetorical itself! You will have spotted the familiar aspects of literary language in it already: e.g. the alliteration of 'fictions only and false hair'. The poet who 'plainly' says something is not plain at all, for in 'My God my King', 'King' is metaphor. If you find the sense of the poem hard to get without recognizing references to Baroque architecture and furniture fashions in the first stanza, seeing that landscape gardening is a central metaphor in the second, and that 'pulling for Prime' refers to drawing cards in a game for the first player, in the third, then you are not responding simply to matters of difficulty created by the historic context of the poem. Rather, you are registering the point that Herbert is in love with complexity.

Take the line 'Shepherds are honest people'. Herbert is thinking no doubt of the ordinary Cotswold shepherd with limited literary skills: hence 'let them sing'; but the reference unpacks, no doubt, a memory of the Biblical shepherds when he said that, the ones that came to the nativity of Christ? They were honest enough, surely. Yet he cannot mean that to write in the honest simple way of a shepherd is an ideal. For seventeenth-century poetry is full of shepherds, in 'pastoral' poetry: and those shepherds belong to a highly stylized convention going back to Theocritus and Virgil, where they are not 'proper' shepherds at all, but allegorical figures, who comment on matters not at all appropriate to the simple life. In pastoral, you do 'catch the sense at two removes', which is an exact description of what happens in reading allegory. Thus Herbert's statement turns also into its reverse. Shepherds may be honest people in pastoral poetry, but they are not like Cotswold shepherds: they are not shepherds at all. The poem goes in two directions at once.

The contradiction is not that Herbert is playing down rhetorical devices while using them: that is an artful rhetorician's trick, similarly employed by Sidney in the first sonnet of *Astrophel to Stella* – 'Fool, said my muse, look in thy heart and write' – where the folly is to look for rhetoric, rather than for personal sincerity. But Herbert, desiring the plain style, has no other recourse than to be rhetorical: can only give four words ('My God, my King') in the plain mode of address. It might be argued that the poem is playful: nonetheless Herbert is also attempting sincerity of feeling towards his God, (which perhaps makes a difference from the way people write love-poems), but the choice to write a poem, to say nothing of the style he does it in, puts him straight back into category of writing 'fiction'. He would like not to write that, as the first line declares, but he cannot avoid it. The poem demonstrates the triumph of metaphor, of tropes.

In Herbert's poem the unconscious surfaces in this slippage of language: its refusal to say what the speaker thinks he means. For a last small example, at the end of the second verse of the *Ode to Melancholy*, Keats tells the reader – or himself – to imprison his mistress' hand when she is angry, and 'let her rave, and feed, deep, deep, upon her peerless eyes'. 'Peerless' seems odd: it means 'unequalled', but I also think it contains the implication of 'what does not peer' (odd for a pair of eyes). The second meaning threatens to undo the whole sense of the line. No doubt the pun was unintentional: but its effect, once pointed out, can only make the line problematic. To talk about Keats's intention is no good: the language is riddled with doubleness, because the signifier has no single inherent meaning, and the language-use thus slides intended meaning away into other statements, into displacements of meaning.

Rhetoric and Its Uses

In identifying all speech as in some ways literary, structured by tropes and figures of speech, Nietzsche stresses that speech is always potentially persuasive, rhetorical. In the last section of this chapter, it is worth turning to rhetoric, to consider it historically. Anglo-Saxon criticism has had little to say about the employment of artificial devices to structure poetic language: the Romantics, after all, insisted on the natural use of language in poetry. But in the time of Plato, rules of how to speak began to receive strong conscious formulation.[9] In the *Phaedrus* (370 BC), Plato attacked through the speeches of Socrates a spurious kind of artificiality in speech and writing that placed persuasiveness above truth. (We will consider this further in the next chapter.) Aristotle, in the *Art of Rhetoric* (330 BC) dealt with the topic as a mode of discourse useful in argument, needing to be taught. But rhetoric became more crucial for the Romans, with whom it was linked to the issue of how to persuade people from a governmental position, and how to establish the rule of law, for which its skill was required. Cicero (106–43 BC), Horace, (65–8 BC) and Quintilian (AD 35–100) are all crucial here. The last named wrote the *Institutio Oratoria* – the education of an orator – which, in ten books, set out the whole basis of style and decorum in language-use. The orator was, for Quintilian, the ideal man: making perfect use of the gift of speech. But whereas Cicero had thought that the subject matter of a speech was indistinguishable from its manner (so that you could not paraphrase a speech), Quintilian split the two, and insisted on the separation of style and matter.

The debate thus initiated has continued. Thus Herbert in his poem believes, like Cicero and, indeed, like Plato before him, in the primacy of matter, not style, which is a position in contrast to Quintilian. (But I have argued that Herbert's writing gives him away – that the whole poem is a conscious performance.) Leavis preferred Donne to Milton precisely for the sense that Donne's style was not self-regarding as was Milton's.

In technical and very Modernist terms, we might say that Cicero believed in the excess of the signified over the signifier; whereas in Quintilian, there is the excess of the signifier over the signified. Can you work out the sense of those terms? Can you compare Cicero or Quintilian more usefully to Nietzsche and to Saussure and to Lacan?

DISCUSSION

If you wish to propose the excess of the signified over the signifier, you are saying that concepts, meaning, come first, and that language – the signifiers – has the task of expressing these concepts. You may think, like Pope, that the ideas are 'what oft was thought', so that poetry leads to single truths. You may argue the contrary case, like Leavis, that poetic language is heuristic: that is, that it reaches out towards intuitions and discoveries not fully conscious to the writer. But either way, you believe in the primary of meaning – that 'words, after speech, reach / Into the silence', (T. S. Eliot, 'Burnt Norton' in *Four Quartets*) and that in the 'silence', there is meaning.

The opposite position is apparent in Nietzsche and Lacan. 'Facts is precisely what there is not, only interpretations.'[10] They hold that all there exists in the text is the play of signifiers, and consider that meaning depends on the way the reader chooses to take that play. In Lacan, the human subject derives identity and meaning from the signifiers that he or she is placed under. There is no pre-existent signified that language tries to catch up on: indeed, as we have seen, meaning is something that can only be generated in the relationship between two signifiers.

Quintilian would not, of course, have gone along with that essentially Modernist and post-Modernist conclusion. (He would certainly have said, without question, that there was truth to be known, beyond the play of language.) Nonetheless, it is no coincidence that Lacan quotes Quintilian. He takes the various figures of speech – tropes – that Quintilian enumerated, and lists them as having to do either with condensation or displacement in discourse. (A trope – a 'turn', literally – Quintilian defines in Book VIII as 'the alteration of a word from its proper meaning to another'. I say more about rhetorical tropes in the Appendix.) Lacan's argument involves the sense that a rhetorical device is not so much a prescription as to how to write persuasively, as an account of the way language characteristically works. There cannot be the expression of a unitary truth within the signifiers that make up a statement, for all those signifiers exist as part of a system of differences, and that immediately sets up signification as dual, not united, not single.

The Use of Rhetoric in Poetry

The Middle Ages looked to Cicero, and an anonymous text, the *Rhetorica ad Herennium*, mistakenly attributed to Cicero, for guidance on rhetoric, the science concerned with how to speak, and it was made the third of the seven liberal arts: above grammar and logic (dialectic). The skills of invention, of the arrangement of material, of memory (crucial for a speaker), of delivery and of style were dwelt on. While rhetoric had meant the study of literature, (for example, Homer) in order to find rules for speech in the classical period, it became identical to poetry itself for the Middle Ages: to write poetry was to write rhetoric. Dante (1265–1321) was to define a poem, in his *De Vulgari Eloquentia* ('Literature in the common tongue') as 'a rhetorical composition set to music': the *ars rhetorica* together with further material on versification, together comprised the *ars poetica* of the period. The Renaissance was to use Quintilian as well, and English Elizabethan poetry comes into being as a conscious rhetorical art, influenced by such textbooks as George Puttenham's *The Art of English Poesie* (1589). In the third book of this, 'Of ornament', Puttenham dealt with tropes: in defining figurative language, he gives one of the earliest English definitions, effectively, of what we are calling, however provisionally, 'literary language': it is 'a novelty of language evidently (and yet not absurdly) estranged from the ordinary habit and manner of our daily talk and writing . . . giving them ornament or efficacy by many manner of alterations in shape, sound, and also in sense, sometime by disorder, or imitation'. 'Estranged' is good in the light of the later emphasis of the Russian Formalists!

Where literature is recognized as a rhetorical art, it is not separated from the art of persuasion, in which it has had, importantly, both a public and political role. The seventeenth century, in Hobbes and Locke, sees a downplaying of the arts of speech: in 1667 the historian of the Royal Society, Thomas Sprat, was to speak of the value of 'a close, naked, natural way of speaking, positive expressions, clear senses, a native easiness, bringing all things as near the mathematical plainness as they can'.[11] Elevated rhetorical style is played down: in the new scientific perception of the seventeenth century, language is required to be closely mimetic of experience, realistic, plain. Though public poetry continues, with Milton, Dryden, Pope, the move is to marginalize poetry from the public

sphere to the private. Rhetoric is driven out, as a conscious art, and
the later eighteenth century sees a literature increasingly private,
meditative, often separated from 'important' political functions,
hurting no one. John Stuart Mill's nineteenth century definition of
poetry becomes symptomatic: it is 'utterance which is not heard but
overheard'. The poet is no longer even Wordsworth's 'man speaking
to men', on this count.

The scientifically-orientated post-Renaissance world in its
positivism has privileged 'truth' as something 'mathematically
plain', and needing, therefore, no demonstration. It is the reverse of
Nietzsche's position, which, of course, attacks it, and the triumph of
an attitude that believes in single, unitary truths, in demonstrable
propositions. The scientific spirit repressed the involvement of a
persuasive language in actually making such statements possible. It
has not seen that its own mathematical plainness is a produce of
language-use: a language that does, covertly, persuade and coerce,
by its terms of reference, by its selection of tropes and metaphors.
(Consider the implications of the metaphors of 'naked' and 'natural'
in Sprat's own formulation.) Raising the question whether there is a
specific 'literary language' keeps from sight the literary/rhetorical
nature of all language: even of scientific. When rhetoric was prac-
tised, the point could be glimpsed – that speech is persuasion. It was
not a point Socrates relished, in the *Phaedrus*.

Yet finally the Modernism of Nietzsche and Saussure needs
stressing: earlier rhetoricians would never have accepted their radical scepticism about reaching to some truth not dependent on
discourse. The example is Aristotle, who, in the *Poetics* defined a
metaphor as 'the application to one thing of a name belonging to
another thing'. In other words, a metaphor implies the pre-existence
of the thing before it is named. Language involves 'troping', – that is,
twisting, turning, moving one figure of speech into another. The
question is what ultimately moves. As Charles Olson, the Modernist
American poet puts it in the middle of his *Maximus* poems, speaking
of an objector to his thoroughly allusive method of writing, arguing
that it is not 'about' anything:

> He sd, "You go all around the subject". And I sd. "I didn't know it was
> a subject". He said, You "twist", and I sd. "I do". He said other
> things. And I didn't say anything.   Letter 15

I leave you to ponder the wit of that, and its style: is it prose or
poetry? (It appears within a volume of poetry.) Doesn't its own
twisting manner evade the scientistic demand for exact description
and exact subject?

6. Meaning and Literary Language

Great literature is simply language charged with meaning to the utmost possible degree.

Ezra Pound: 'How to Read'

Compare the ending of these two novels. First comes Joyce's *Portrait of the Artist as a Young Man*, which, though published in 1914–15 was written before Lawrence's *Sons and Lovers* (1913), the second extract. In the comparison, concentrate on the differences in writing and attitudes towards language. In the light of the last chapter, which passage seems more openly rhetorical? Which draws attention to the priority of the signifier more? It will help to know that in the first of these two 'autobiographical' pieces, Stephen Dedalus about to leave his mother and Ireland makes an entry in his diary; in the second, the narrator recounts Paul Morel's thoughts and actions impelled by the memory of his dead mother.

April 26. Mother is putting my new secondhand clothes in order. She prays, she says, that I may learn in my own life and away from home and friends what the heart is and what it feels. So be it. Welcome, O life! I go to encounter for the millionth time the reality of experience and to forge in the smithy of my soul the uncreated conscience of my race.
April 27. Old father, old artificer, stand me now and ever in good stead.

. . . So much, and himself, infinitesimal, at the core a nothingness, and yet not nothing.
'Mother!', he whimpered – 'mother!'
She was the only thing that held him up, himself, amid all this. And she was gone, intermingled herself. He wanted her to touch him, have him alongside with her.
But no, he would not give in. Turning sharply, he walked towards the city's gold phosphorescence. His fists were shut, his mouth set fast.

He would not take that direction, to the darkness, to follow her. He
walked towards the faintly humming, glowing town, quickly.

DISCUSSION

I think that although the passage from *Sons and Lovers* is fairly
rhetorical – we note how Paul Morel seems to strike a pose in it, both
physically, and as the narrator presents his attitudes to us – the Joyce
passage is in touch with language as a self-conscious game, with
words to be played with. I wonder if, like me, you were surprised that
the Lawrence came later. Joyce's work has such a different feel about
it in its use of language. The ironies are strong in it, and it is obviously
rhetorical, while also mocking rhetoric. Look at the witty oxymoron
of 'new secondhand', and the ironising of attitudes: of the mother –
'she prays, she says' – note the rhyme, and the double meaning: she
says she prays, and she prays and tells me about it: and note the
self-ironising: in the pose struck – 'So be it. Welcome, O life!'. In
contrast, the Lawrence piece takes itself much more solemnly. In
fact, Joyce's word 'forge' is crucial: for it means both 'make' and
'make up', just as in the next line, 'artificer' means both 'maker' and
'liar'. (The reference to the old father is to Daedalus, which means
'artful', an etymology Joyce would have known. Daedalus was a
smith and craftsman, and made wings for himself and his son to fly
out of Crete: as Stephen is quitting Dublin. But Icarus' wings did not
stand him in good stead, and part of the irony lies here.)
    The effect of the references to forging and lying creates a new
category – that of the writer as liar. Whereas the nineteenth-century
novel – the 'classic realist text' has within it the illusion that a truth is
being worked away at by the writer, here there is no conviction that
the text can, necessarily, say anything.
    Lawrence's novel is a sheer contrast. The voice in the narrative
identifies closely with Paul Morel, and assumes that it knows what is
going on inside his mind: it is difficult, indeed, to know whether the
voice is that of a narrator or of Paul himself. There is a certain poetic
heightening to the narrative: 'gold phosphorescence' – 'faintly humming': these ideas may be connected metonymically (as in the rhythm
of 'his fists were shut, his mouth set fast'), and 'quickly' may suggest
that Paul is among the quick (alive), not the dead, as his mother is,
but the meaning here does not give way to language, to the 'play of
the signifier', as it does with Joyce.
    The difference between Joyce and Lawrence is in the sense of
where meaning resides. In the Lawrence extract, there is a strong
feeling that we are being told: how do we know that Paul Morel does
not give in to suicidal tendencies? Simply on the say-so of the

narrator, who is presumed to know because of the *authority* invested in the idea of the *author*. No such illusions underpin Joyce's work. It is as though Joyce were aware of Saussure, and of the arguments put forward about the arbitrary nature of the signifier, and the impossibility of fixing a meaning within a chain of signifiers.

Lawrence's writing assumes a fit between plain speech and meaning: though there are elements of the Modernist within him, he belongs to a tradition that insists on the naturalness of writing and the possibility of presenting a reality that can be empirically validated by the reader. The opposition between Lawrence's position and Joyce's (the Realist versus Formalist position, it might be described otherwise) is basic, and it continues in debates about the nature of language. In this chapter, I want to consider how one strain of Modernist and more recent writing has argued for the use of literary language to overturn conventional meanings. It is here that Joyce belongs, writing, as he does, a prose that disrupts a clear sense of communication between writer and reader. The literary language asked for here has a utopist, sometimes political (specifically, at times, feminist) aim behind it – to create new meanings, new possibilities. But we begin with Jacques Derrida, (born 1930) a philosopher – or perhaps anti-philosopher – strongly indebted to Nietzsche and Saussure and Heidegger, and to his work on the impossibility of attaching meaning to writing.

Freeing the Text – Derrida

Derrida's work, standing, as he puts it, 'on the margins of philosophy', attacks Western traditions of thought, beginning with Plato, that take the view that writing approaches, or can approach, whatever lies outside the play of signifiers. Plato, in the *Phaedrus*, a treatise devoted to attacking rhetoric, and writing (a medium favoured by the then contemporary rhetoricians), prefers speech, and makes Socrates say so. Look at what Socrates tells the young Phaedrus, and in the light of what was said about rhetoric in the last chapter, decide what Plato stands for, and what his attitude to 'literary language', if he could imagine such a thing, would be:

> To believe . . . that a written composition on any subject must be to a large extent the creation of fancy; that nothing worth serious attention has ever been written in prose or verse . . . that even the best of such compositions can do no more than help the memory of those who already know; whereas lucidity and finality and serious importance are to be found only in words spoken by way of instruction, or . . . written on the soul of the hearer to enable him to learn about the right, the beautiful and the good . . . to realize that such spoken truths are to

be reckoned a man's legitimate sons . . . to believe all this, I say, and to let all else go, is to be the sort of man, Phaedrus, that you and I might well pray that we may both become.[1]

DISCUSSION

Clearly, Plato would believe in 'the excess of the signified over the signifier', and for the view that so much language is just decoration, and that what is needed is articulation of pure truth.

But why does he prefer speaking to writing? Because, Derrida answers, there is the myth of a personal presence established in speech. If I talk to you, you can hear my tone of voice, you can ask me to repeat myself, and you can get a sense that you know what sort of person I am. In writing, you can puzzle for ages over what might be meant by something; and there is no way of checking, particularly if the author has died. But Derrida would say that this idea of 'presence' is indeed a myth, nothing else: that just because speech is taking place, that does not make the subject speaking autonomous and real. Speech and meaning in speech (and here he follows Saussure) are a matter of convention only: speech, like writing, is a set of marks, except that they are made in the air, not on paper. And if I repeat myself, I do not clarify matters, for then I make another statement, which may be a metalingual one. No one statement can mean the same as another. They are different, and two things that are different are not the same: indeed, nothing can be the same, for the word 'same' already implies difference.

For Derrida, the idea of some original presence, or truth-finding expression in language, is the profound error of Western thought and, he would add, it belongs to a tradition that wishes to create a hierarchy of absolute truths that actually only have a purely mythical basis. Instead, Derrida illustrates the point that everything in language is riven by what he terms *différance* – a neologism that combines the meanings of 'differ' and 'to defer'. In the chain of signifiers that make up, say, a poem, each word gains its meaning only by its difference from the next, and that sense of difference is multiplied by the next signifier, and so on, and thus meaning never resides in any one part of the text, but is rather always 'deferred'. In the text there is a 'dissemination' of the signifier ('seme' is Greek: Derrida puns in suggesting that its significance is plural, generative and broadcast like seed. A reader cannot say 'this is what the poem means'; nor say 'this is what the author meant', for language – whether spoken or written – will disallow any intention – which was, in any case, presumably expressed in some other metalanguage.

Derrida, in a reading of the *Phaedrus* called 'Plato's Pharmacy',[2] points to the irony that Plato writes down the presumably fictional words of the dead Socrates: attacking writing by writing it. The intention, to dismiss writing, is 'deconstructed' by its mode of appearance in language: Socrates's speech in Plato's writing is still a 'creation of fancy'. It is not clear what Plato is trying to do to Socrates: kill him off (one meaning of *pharmakon* in Greek is 'poison'), or revive his authority – the other meaning of the word is 'medicine'. If you take the text in one way, writing is killed stone-dead by the voice of Socrates – if you take it another, Socrates is killed off, and the text effectively validates rhetoric and writing. The element of undecidability between two meanings is vital: the issue, presents similarities to the discussion of Herbert's poem, *Jordan (1)*.

This position – or these positions – render impossible unitary, univalent meaning: the similarity with Bakhtin's argument (Chapter 3) should be noted. Criticism, in the name of 'relevance' and 'disciplined response' – both favourite terms of Leavis, for instance – will impose their own 'closure' on the text by deciding that such-and-such is its right interpretation: but that only raises the question as to why the critic wishes to read the text thus: from what ideological position he or she is coming from, by what process of 'secondary revision' (to return to Freud on dreams), the multivalent signifiers of the text have been made to yield what looks a perfectly consistent sense. The author of the text is no longer (as in Lawrence) to be presumed the controlling voice speaking from a deep intention; rather, Roland Barthes writes an essay called 'The death of the author'. In some ways, we have returned to Stanley Fish's argument: to read a text as literature becomes the choice of the reader (though the choice is not made by the reader, but by the pressures that decide that one text is literature, and another is not). The position is adopted by Jonathan Culler in *Structuralist Poetics* that literariness is in the eye of the reader: what needs examining is not the text for some essentialist 'literary language', but the 'literary competence' of the reader. (We discussed this position briefly as it touches Stanley Fish, in Chapter 4.) In her book *The Language Poets Use* (1962), Winifred Nowottny begins by defining a verbal structure as literary 'if it presents its topic at more than one level of presentation at the same time – or, alternatively, if one and the same utterance has more than one function in the structure of meaning in which it occurs'. Derrida's position, in contrast, suggests that there is no agreed structure of meaning for a linguistic structure: to determine a function is to decide that the text will be read in this way or that. 'All reading is misreading', Paul de Man (closely associated with Derrida) has said. We are back to *The Bible Designed to Be Read as*

Literature. To decide to read a text in any one way immediately dictates how much referential 'truth' can be expected from it.

Derrida, speaking of his approach, calls it 'plus d'une langue'.[3] The French here contains a pun: it is 'both more than a language' and 'no more of *a* language'. If you go back to the issues of Chapter 2, you will see how much emphasis was laid by Coleridge and others on the right words in the right places. The critics of Chapter 2, without exception, have little room for translation, regarding it as a poor second-best for the original language, which incarnates a unique perception that does not translate. Derrida's work sees that as mystificatory: making a fetish out of a language, and implying that far from a poem, for example, only being able to exist in one mode, in its organic form, it benefits from the plurality of translation: a text needs not the purity of one language, with its specific emphases, but needs several. Significantly, one writer who appears frequently in Derrida's work is Joyce: here the play of several languages, and the playing between languages is obviously crucial, especially in *Finnegans Wake*. And Derrida's *Glas* (1974) 'out-Joyces' Joyce in its play of languages to discuss Hegel and Genet simultaneously: here all divisions between 'literature', 'criticism' and 'philosophy' collapse.

Implications for Literary Language

What does Derrida's work suggest for a discussion of literary language? He has refused any sense of a determinate purpose being seen in a text: taking issue here with John Searle,[4] the American 'speech-act' theorist, for whom any utterance is *locutionary* (said in words and sounds), *propositional* (attributing a property to a referent outside language), and *illocutionary* – an act of stating, of promising, or questioning, or even marrying, as in 'I do' in one context. Speech here is purposive: Searle agrees with Austin, who was mentioned in the last chapter, and it includes therefore a specific type of person – the person who receives the message. Derrida will have none of this. A text remains just that: a text. There is no sense in reading, say, philosophy, in another way from the way we take 'literature'. 'Literary language' is a pleonasm, then: all language is literary, because it is all mere writing (the earlier meaning of 'literary'), and it can all be read for the guileful, ambiguous and indeterminate uses of language that literature employs. We broaden the scope of discussion: 'what is literary language?' is not a question to be asked merely by those who study 'literature': it affects those who write history, philosophy, political science or science itself.

At this point, let us return to a very specific literary example, and one which does not look at all like Joyce, or anything Modernist, or even ambiguous. How would Derrida's arguments help with, say, Augustan poetry? Take this example from Doctor Johnson's poem, *The Vanity of Human Wishes*, about which T. S. Eliot wrote that 'these lines, especially the first two, with their just inevitable sequence of *barren*, *petty* and *dubious*, still seem to me the finest that have ever been written in that particular idiom'.[5] How is Eliot's position in contrast to Derrida? What words would you use to characterize the kind of writing here? Can you see any way in which Derrida's work could get a toe-hold on writing as simple and plain as this? (These four lines describe the dismal ending, as a prisoner, of the proud Charles XII of Sweden, in 1718):

> His fall was destin'd to a barren strand,
> A petty fortress and a dubious hand;
> He left the name, at which the world grew pale
> To point a moral, or adorn a tale.

DISCUSSION

Johnson's lines work by their strict logic: the man's fall compared to what happened to his name: the fall itself going in an ordered, gradually contracting sequence, from the place to the metonymy of the 'hand' (belonging to the murderer). Johnson's mocking point is that all the man was finally good for was to provide an illustration for a 'tale' told by himself: it is a descent into *bathos*, an anti-climax indeed. The words I would use to describe the lines would be *prosaic* (not a criticism!), ordered, neat and epigrammatical, and utterly steady in structure: look at the positions of the alliterations, (petty and point) for instance. Eliot would suggest that these lines could not be put differently without loss.

But the whole tone is that of good, careful prose, despite the verse format. It aims at single meaning, at lack of ambiguity. Derrida's interest is a contrary one, it has to do with the erasure of that single sense, and the discovery of plurality. However, the point that a critic influenced by Derrida's 'deconstruction' would make is that Johnson's text undoes its pretensions to single meaning by being 'literary': that is, poetic, in verse form. The tale is 'adorned' by more than just the history of Charles XII getting a straightforward narration. It is played with by the author, too. A poem called *The Vanity of Human Wishes* contains its own pride, despite its title, both in the very confidence involved in writing it, and in that Charles XII is finally declared by implication, inferior to the writer of the 'tale', and the writer plays with this point in moving the narration thus towards its climax. Indeed, if this conviction of his own uncompromised ability were not somewhere within the poem, it would have been impossible to write it at all. However single minded the words (though I wonder what the ambiguous time-sequence of 'at which the world grew pale' is: during the man's life? (He was a conqueror. Or after his death, when people discover Johnson has used him in his poem?) there is still a structural doubleness, which reveals 'literariness' to be ambiguity, undecidability.

Effectively, all texts become literary; that is, they can be taken that way. In his book on Nietzsche, *Spurs*, Derrida has some amusing pages on a line of Nietzsche's found amongst his papers: 'I have forgotten my umbrella'. The plurality of interpretations given to this only emphasizes that it is the existence of the all-important frame of reference that gives any decidability about how any sentence or phrase is taken. You have to set a boundary around something, and declare it 'literary': then it will be read as such. But if literature were to lose its boundaries, that might provide something liberating: for all the preferred readings that put one text into the category of literature and another into a separate one, reinforce what Derrida calls a 'violent hierarchy'[6] (*Positions*, (Chicago, 1981) p. 41). In this hierarchy, certain meanings have been used, often enough, as the excuse to maintain them in a structure of dominance. In other words, there is a repressive force at work in the way that texts are read for a single, or dominant meaning.

The Pleasure of the Text

We have used the expression, 'the excess of the signifier over the signified', and the post-structuralist writers mentioned (Barthes, Lacan, Derrida) have been brought together for their sense of this and their refusal of a deep meaning or truth emerging from the signifier. Meaning is secured by a repression of difference within the chain of signifiers; a refusal to see that within the rhetorical tropes of language, there is an opacity which effectively undoes illusions of single meaning. Freud spoke about the 'return of the repressed' – in dreams, for example, while Barthes similarly speaks about the 'return of the different' in the text – there for all to see, but only perceived by re-reading, by reading in a manner that refuses to take the text in the manner that the author, the arch-censor, wishes.

Barthes proposes, then, the text itself, as something that by its play of signification banishes the author and the reader's desire to take in a single meaning. He asks for 'the birth of the reader', as the creative figure liberated from textual 'authority'. The text of *jouissance* (as over against socially acceptable *plaisir* – pleasure) – is what he looks for: *jouissance* includes the idea of sexual orgasm, which, as *la petite mort* – the little death – radically disconfirms the self, and can't be described, only experienced. What is sought is a text which, through its linguistic, surface play, baffles and disconfirms the self that believes in meaning.

Literary language as the play of 'disseminated' signifiers gives birth to this pleasure. Earlier, when Modernism was discussed, it was seen that in France, post-Flaubert writers were seen working in a way that drew attention to the language itself, as something existing in its own being. Thus, take Mallarmé's sonnet, 'Ses purs ongles'. Its general theme may be that of anguish, but it is, strictly, designed to baffle attempts to find meaning. Here is its second verse, with my translation:

> Sur les crédences, au salon vide: nul ptyx,
> Aboli bibelot d'inanité sonore,
> (Car le Maître est allé puiser des pleurs au Styx
> Avec ce seul objet dont le Néant s'honore).

(On the sideboards, in the empty room: no ptyx, abolished knick-knacks of sonorous emptiness, (for the Master has gone to draw tears from the Styx, with this single object that Nothingness takes pride in).

Michael Riffaterre, whose work you will recall from the end of Chapter 4, in discussing this poem sees the stanza as constructed round the matrix of 'emptiness': the 'salon vide' (empty room) inspires five variations on that theme: there is no owner, and there is no ptyx, no knick-knacks (look at the construction of the words 'aboli bibelot': even if you know no French, you will see the way the words mirror each other); sonorous emptiness, and one object that Nothingness honours. And what about the word 'ptyx'? Mallarmé boasted that it was a word unknown in any language. So not only is there no ptyx, but even if there were it would still mean there was nothing.

The text quite simply abolishes the real world, saying effectively that the supreme reality is that to be found in the poem, within language. But to turn to a word like 'ptyx' is to find that there is no meaning there either: all that can be rested on is the word as material sign. For there is nothing to be found in the room. (In Italian that would be a pun, for a stanza means both a verse and a room.) If you recall the argument of Lacan, that the insertion of the human into the symbolic order of language involves displacement and misnaming of the subject so constituted, you might argue that this poem over-throws the symbolic order; subverts it: that it sets out as though it meant something, but strictly, it means nothing at all. But it still generates – perhaps hauntingly – images: it produces a 'significance', not a meaning. There is no real English equivalent word for this term, but its importance is crucial.

The term comes from Julia Kristeva, (born 1941) the Bulgarian by origin feminist critic who has worked in France in the area of semiotics. Again, we touched on her work at the end of Chapter 4, for the important concept of 'intertextuality' – the view that 'texts smell of other texts', which she derived from Bakhtin's writing. Her evocation is of a poetic/literary language that escapes somehow the straitjacket of unitary meaning imposed by the 'symbolic order'. She concentrates on the text where there is the production of 'sig-nifiance', a less specific enlargement of sense. Much of her work relates to Lacanian psychoanalysis. Thus she distinguishes between the *semiotic* and the *symbolic* states: the first of which is connected to the Mother, and to the Imaginary state, where the infant is in direct communication with the other, who is not thought of as separate, other in that sense, but as a part of the self. The second is attached to the entry into language, where the Imaginary is broken, and the child is caught in a world of precise meanings and grammatical and social constraints. We have already seen how language deforms the subject, in Lacan's terms. The literary text Kristeva is interested in breaks with the symbolic order. Her definition of poetic language is relevant in the context of Barthes and Derrida. For her,

> literary practice is seen as exploration and discovery of the possibil-
> ities of language, as an activity that liberates the script from a number
> of linguistic, psychic and social networks, as a dynamic that breaks up
> the inertia of language habits and grants linguists the unique possibil-
> ity of studying the *becoming* of the signification of signs.[7]

It sounds like another form of defamiliarization. What is entailed in this definition?

There is no sense, in Kristeva's work, as you will have noticed from such verbs as 'liberates' and 'breaks up', that ordinary speech is itself creative. If it does create, that is beside the point, effectively. Rather, being put into language thrusts you into the midst of disparate texts that construct you, and make you speak them. The human subject – it is important to stress that the female subject is strongly involved – is caught between 'intertexts', and 'intertextual-ity' is her term for the condition both people and literary texts subsist in: both only make sense because they are held in a network of other discourses. 'Every text is from the outset under the jurisdiction of other discourses which impose a universe on it', (*Revolution*, pp. 338–9). The text receives its meaning from other texts. We know, for example, how to read a detective novel because we have read others, and know what value to attach to each of the narrative moves, for instance. If you just read one with no sense of the genre it belongs to, you would get in a muddle for you would not see that its whole form is structured by other texts. It has been coded already: just as, Kristeva argues, the human subject is thoroughly coded.

Implicit in Kristeva's sense of the text yielding not a specific meaning, but releasing 'signifiance', just as with Barthes' emphasis on the unsettling 'jouissance' produced from the text that is only partly intelligible (like the Mallarmé), is the desire to subvert hierarchies of established meanings. The aim is to disrupt the Symbolic, social order: to return to something analogous to the 'semiotic' condition, that active process where feelings and signifiance are released in an overflow of pleasure – *jouissance*. Here conceptualization fails: we move between meanings, as it were, like jazz musicians moving between the white notes on the keyboard. And 'signifiance' is ongoing, not static or fixed. I think this is what Kristeva means when she speaks of the 'becoming of the signification of signs': where signs do not quite mean, but signify – expand vision and thought.

Literary Language and 'Signifiance'

We are moving towards a sense that there may be an important function for language – to become poetic/literary in order to generate new possibilities of signifiance. Kristeva with her highly theorized feminism which uses Derrida and Lacan, sounds very far from T. S. Eliot, but Eliot writes of the area 'where language fails, though meanings still exist', which implies that words may well prove obdurate to the flow of possibilities that exist, and that could be brought to consciousness. Writing on the 'auditory imagination', he described 'the feeling for syllable and rhythm, penetrating far below the conscious levels of thought and feeling', and claimed to know that 'a poem, a passage of a poem may tend to realize itself first as a particular rhythm before it reaches expression in words, and that this rhythm may bring to birth the idea and the image'.[8] Here is the suggestion that the poem begins almost as a somatic pressure, linked to the body and its pulsions, the linking of words in poetic form coming later.

A comment of Virginia Woolf's may help, where she seems to put rhythm above words. 'Now this is very profound, what rhythm is, and goes far deeper than words. A sight, an emotion, creates this wave in the mind, long before it makes words to fit it' (letter of 16 March, 1926). Bodily pulsions, 'waves' (we may compare Kristeva's sense of the semiotic), may generate words to follow them and seek to imitate them – and these feelings may well imply that the words will be inadequate, that their stated sense may be much less import-ant than their reverberations, the way that they 'echo / Thus, in your mind' ('Burnt Norton', *Four Quartets*). Leavis, too, insisted in a notable exchange with René Wellek that poetry was unparaphras-able. There are details of his argument that go in different direction from what is at issue here, the difference between meaning and *significance*, but there is a link too.

A suggestion of D. W. Harding, a critic closely associated with Leavis, may help; he writes on Isaac Rosenberg, the war poet:

> 'Clothing a thought in language' ... seems a fair metaphorical description of much speaking and writing. Of Rosenberg's work it would be misleading. He ... brought language to bear on the incipient thought at an earlier stage of its development. Instead of the emerging idea being racked slightly so as to fit a more familiar approximation of itself, and words found for *that*, Rosenberg let it manipulate words almost from the beginning, often without insisting on the controls of logic and intelligibility.[9]

To the first type of writing belongs *The Vanity of Human Wishes* which we looked at above. To what extent we can bring together such voices as Eliot, Leavis, Harding and Woolf with Kristeva, Barthes, and Derrida is something that I leave you to consider. They have been strongly opposed by critics taking up sides in debates on the nature of literature: the English voices here quoted standing for an old-style humanism, (this may not apply to Woolf), which is refuted by the post-structuralist focus on the subject coming into play through being constituted by a language sodden in ideological assumptions. I will come back to this problem in Chapter 7, in terms of the opposition of these names: recognizing that a confrontation between them is at the heart of this book's argument.

Harding's argument might be applied to this poem of William Empson's, an example of English Modernism, called 'Let it go'. Note that however opaque the poem is as to 'meaning', it has very strong controls of form: indeed, within that tension between tight form and contradictoriness in sense, significance is generated.

> It is this deep blankness is the real thing strange.
>   The more things happen to you, the more you can't
>   Tell or remember even what they were.
>
> The contradictions cover such a range.
>   The talk would talk and go so far aslant.
>   You don't want madhouse and the whole thing there.

The poem refuses, despite the strong use of colloquialisms ('real thing strange', 'whole thing there') and despite its appearance of giving a propositional truth, the idea of stateable truth, attacking the desire for consciously articulated meaning, with the feeling that that way madness lies. A sense of the slide into endless metonymies and metaphors, ('the talk would talk'), horrifies Empson. Yet though I find the language haunting here in its implications, 'deep blankness' for instance, and in that sense it bears out Harding's point, it is a poem deliberately very controlled in its use of language, and we would have to look elsewhere for a text less cerebral, one that has to do, in Kristeva's emphasis, with the body, or with the semiotic.

As an example of a text that oscillates between the stated sense of language, and the feeling that it obeys a rhythmic pull which is separable from that and which cannot be rendered in terms of meaning, consider this extract from the Scottish writer Lewis Grassic Gibbon, whose *A Scots Quair*, (1934) about Chris Guthrie, uses an idiosyncratic, artificial form of Scots speech throughout. In this early passage, the young Chris' education is described:

> So that was Chris and her reading and schooling, two Chrisses there were that fought for her heart and tormented her. You hated the land and the coarse speak of the folk and learning was brave and fine one day and the next you'd waken with the peewits crying across the hills, deep and deep, crying in the heart of you and the smell of the earth in your face, almost you'd cry for that, the beauty of it and the sweetness of the Scottish lands and skies. You saw their faces in firelight, father's and mother's and the neighbours', before the lamps lit up, tired and kind, faces dear and close to you, you wanted the words they'd known and used, forgotten in the far-off youngness of their lives, Scots words to tell to your heart, how they wrung it and held it, the toil of their days and unendingly their fight. And the next minute that passed from you, you were English, back to the English words so sharp and clean and true – for a while, for a while, till they slid so smooth from your throat you knew they could never say anything that was worth the saying at all.
>
> ('Sunset Song' – 'Ploughing', Pan edition, 1981, p. 32)

DISCUSSION

This passage, like so much in *A Scots Quair* dramatizes the difficulties of how to speak. Standard English might here represent the 'symbolic order' (dominant, and in control of preferred political meanings), into which Chris is half-willingly being inserted, and the rejection of it is crucial – for its ability to conceptualize, to interpret, to remove 'signifiance'. Gibbon writes a deliberately heightened form of speech which is Scots in derivation, but which at the same time works against ordinary grammatical construction, and uses the Scots in a very supple way. We cannot be sure who is speaking: who is the 'you' – the narrator talking to Chris? Chris to herself or someone else? The narrator about everybody? The break-up of strict logical sense here is also found in the choice of words – e.g. 'unendingly their fight'. The rhythmic repetitions (for instance, from 'and the next you'd waken' to the end of the sentence) carry a surge, a strong pulse, that the words try to follow.

Barthes would have liked the stress on the non-physicality of English as the dominant discourse that has to be resisted. In *Image: Music: Text*, he writes on 'the grain of the voice', stressing the need for a language which has a strong physical grain, which involves the body in its articulation. A language which is thus gritty and that strongly evokes the energies of the body deflects attention from the message with its 'spiritual', non-physical value, and thus attacks the view that meaning is somehow pure and transcendent, and, above all, single.

Thus the artificial language adopted here, in opposition to conventional English, is deliberately literary, calling attention to the play of signifiers, not working in a purely rational sense. For a last example, take Bob Dylan's lyric, the last verse of 'Mr Tambourine Man':

> Then take me disappearin' down the smoke rings of my mind,
> Down the foggy ruins of time, far past the frozen leaves,
> The haunted, frightened trees, out to the windy beach,
> Far from the twisted reach of crazy sorrow.
> Yes, to dance beneath the diamond sky with one hand waving free
> Silhouetted by the sea, circled by the circus sands,
> With all memory and fate driven deep beneath the waves,
> Let me forget about today until tomorrow.

Both lyric and mode of writing reach away from publicly certifiable 'meaning' to *signifiance*. Of course, the writing can be considered formalistically, (consider the assonantal and symmetrical movement of the words 'mind', 'time', 'leaves', 'trees', 'beach', 'reach' (a pun here, since a reach is an area of beach), 'free', 'sea'; consider the shift from 'waving' to 'waves'. But since everyone who remembers the 1960s will know this as a lyric, consider how the effect of hearing it sung, with its onward compulsion in the music, drives out the need to consider formal meaning, and generates its own 'semiotic' value. The Dylan lyric returns us to pleasure in literary language as also aurally based, to do with sound as well as sense, but with clear, dominant sense held in suspension.

Summary

To encapsulate in little where Derrida's work serves, heavily Nietzschean and Freudian/Lacanian as it is, we must follow how 'deconstruction' attacks unitary, single meaning in the text – or even plural, subtly nuanced ambiguous meanings – since it refuses the concept of the autonomy of the subject that creates the text. In Derrida, the subject is already formed through a rhetoric within language-structures that in any case means that thought exists as subject to the tropes and figures that make up language: but in any case, 'thought' is not separable from those tropes; there is no subject that thinks outside the range of those figures. Thus to put a frame around one language-type and call this 'literary' is a matter of wishing to impose a passe-partout on utterance, and to try to abstract a clear line of thought from it: an illusion, of course.

I say 'of course', though recognizing that this fundamentally challenges a humanistic criticism which begins with the priority of the author, with the concept of intention as valuable, with moral seriousness, and so on. Derrida's work affronts a criticism that may go so far as to believe, (inspired by Modernism) that the writer should cede the initiative to words, and should allow for a play of meanings within the text – may even use that play to subvert established meaning and conventional thought. There is a genuine divide here. But it will be conceded that to say that the text cannot be deemed 'meaningful' or 'literary' even, in one way only, does not prevent a text having an impact; allows for possibilities to come through which in their suggestiveness continue to resonate. In the last chapter, we will examine this via Paul de Man and Heidegger, and specifically through James Joyce, as well as through feminist theory.

7. Some Conclusions

> Between form and content, between sound and meaning, between the
> poem and the state of poetry, a symmetry is manifested, an equality of
> importance, value and power, that is not in prose; it is opposed to the
> law of prose – which decrees the inequality of language's two constitu-
> ents. The essential principle of the poetic process – that is, of the
> conditions of production of the poetic state by the word – is, to my
> mind, this harmonic exchange between expression and impression.
>
> Paul Valéry, *Works*, translated Josué Harari

In our consideration of 'What is literary language?' we have explored
how the term has been used during this century as a method of trying
to define some essential quality within literature. But one conclusion
that has been proposed in the course of the last two chapters would
deny any validity to the category 'literature', since there can be no
marker that distinguishes between forms of utterance, literary or
otherwise: all texts embody rhetorical strategies, and literary devices
are enshrined within the whole way in which language works
through the speaker. If, then, returning to Chapter 1, the question
was asked, 'Is there a literary language?' the answer, I believe, would
have to be 'No'; there is no inherent quality of language that you
could spot a mile off, and say that this belongs to art or 'literature',
and is therefore to be privileged is some way or other. It is not even
clear that if you could say it belonged to 'art' it would then become,
of necessity, worthy of attention. Whose art? Elitist or popular art,
for a start?

Further, the concept of a 'literary language', such as the one
recognized by literary theorists in France, during the middle of the
seventeenth century (and which Barthes argued had gone after 1850)
may be seen as reactionary, licensing the idea of fixed, unchanging
meanings to works of literature. For if 'literary language' remains
unaltered, then the relevant texts could be claimed to have an
unchanging, unitary meaning too. This point was made by Raymond
Picard in his *Nouvelle Critique ou Nouvelle Imposture* (1965),
attacking Roland Barthes' readings of Racine, and arguing that there

could be one single reading of Racine's plays. Barthes' response (in *Critique et verité*, 1966) to Picard insists that the idea of a literary language is destructive insofar as it licenses the view that meanings of works are not dependent upon historical moments, not relative to cultural conditions. 'Each historical moment', Barthes writes, 'may think that it has isolated the canonical meaning for a work, but one only needs to expand one's view of history a bit to transform this singular meaning into plural meanings, and the closed work into an open work' (p. 50).

Literature, Literary Language and History

But deciding that there is no inherent property of language that makes it literary does not mean to say that in historical terms there is no relevance to the term 'literary language', since there have been historical periods where people believed they were writing, or reading, 'literature', and the determinations that prompted them to think that, and what they discerned in the writing, need investigation. Could Sidney's *Apologie for Poetrie* have existed without the sense of some added greatness in poetry that sets it aside from philosophy or history? Inherited notions about 'literature' have had profound ideological effects on the present, and these have to be examined when we speak about that body of texts, held to have 'literary' features in common, that constitute literature.

Further, it is not to be assumed that all uses of language are the same. Would it not be merely formalistic to say that, because advertising slogans use rhetorical devices, they are equivalent to a lyric poem? In *Ulysses*, Joyce uses advertising devices playfully; and as a reminder of how much they construct our *langue*, our frames of reference, as when Mr Bloom sees in the paper:

> What is home without
> Plumtree's Potted Meat?
> Incomplete.
> With it an abode of bliss.

At the least, the difference lies in intention: the advertising jingle here is literary, in that it uses poetic devices, but it does not generate significance, or if it does, does so quite beyond the ideological position that has occasioned it. Language used in such a way as to open up meaning, we may call what we like; but there seems value in saying that it is important that some language uses are capable of questioning conventional ways of employing the *langue* – as we discussed towards the end of the last chapter – just as other texts confirm a dominant ideology.

But before pursuing that theme, we must see how American deconstruction takes issue with the idea that language in literature can ever further any ends – political, moral, religious – at all. The argument runs that, if all literature comes down to texts made from other texts (just as life does, a point made by quoting advertising in *Ulysses*), and if each text depends on another, then, to be pessimistic, it might be said to be all repetition, rephrasing the same material again and again, only in different voices. Nothing can ever get said. That position would induce a kind of despair and a political quietism. One of the critics most associated with this position was Paul de Man, the late Belgian born American critic much influenced, philosophically, by Derrida, and part of a group known, informally, as the 'Yale school of deconstruction'. He stresses the literary nature of all discourse, as Nietzsche does, but he adds to that the sense that literature is qualitatively different from other forms of discourse in its self-consciousness. In *Blindness and Insight* (New York, 1971), he contends that literature begins 'on the far side' of the knowledge proclaimed by deconstruction and refused by 'ordinary language', that 'sign and meaning can never coincide'. What is de Man saying here about the literary? Do you agree with it or not?

> The self-reflecting mirror effect by means of which a work of fiction asserts, by its very existence, its separation from empirical reality, its divergence, as a sign, from a meaning that depends for its existence on the constitutive activity of this sign, characterizes the work of art in its essence. It is always against the explicit assertion of the writer that readers degrade the fiction by confusing it with a reality from which it has forever taken leave.
>
> (p. 17)

DISCUSSION

De Man wants to contend that the literary can be defined by its lack of pretence that it describes reality: he says, it is 'the only form of language free from the fallacy of unmediated expression': free from the idea that it does mirror reality. If it were unmediated expression, it would be passing itself off as absolutely natural, as true. But de Man contends, in contrast, that the literary always draws attention to its signifying practice, so that it is never trying to bring signifiers and signifieds together simply. Effectively, texts deconstruct themselves by drawing attention to their rhetorical devices. Thus 'we call "literary" in the full sense of the term any text that implicitly or explicitly signifies its own rhetorical mode and prefigures its own misunderstanding as the correlative of its rhetorical nature; that is, of its "rhetoricity"' (*Blindness and Insight*, p. 136). He elsewhere quotes Monroe Beardsley, the New Critic, saying 'that literary language is characterized by being "distinctly above the norm in ratio of implicit (or I would say rhetorical) to explicit meaning"'.[1] Thus readers go astray in taking, say, Dickens's *Bleak House* – described by J. Hillis Miller, another of the Yale school, as 'a document about the interpretation of documents' (introduction to the Penguin edition) – as though it reflected the England and London of 1852. Instead, the world of *Bleak House* is self-referential, and it is only confusing when readers start asking how faithfully Dickens was recording what London was 'really' like.

Now the word 'reflect' poses critical problems, but this definition of the literary suggests that over in one corner we have real life, and over in the other, the literary text, and the two never meet. Nor is there really a possibility of literature commenting on ordinary language, since it is essential to de Man's form of deconstruction that the text contains its negation within itself – its *différance* in Derrida's terms, that which defers meaning, and that causes meaning to be dual, a matter of difference. All that is possible is for a text to recognize this, and to question its own function.[2]

But, for de Man, self-reflexiveness characterizes all literary writing. He holds that metaphor suspends meaning, for example: it does not signify in a definite manner; rather it avoids unitary sense. In *Allegories of Reading*, while equating 'the rhetorical, figural potential of language with literature itself', he argues that 'rhetoric actually suspends logic and opens up vertiginous possibilities of referential aberration . . .' (p. 10). Consider how rhetoric is deployed here in a different sense from what it had in Chapter 4. Here it is not in the service of public persuasion; rather, it prevents or delays the appearance of meaning in the private sphere of the single, lonely writer!

I would want to disagree with de Man on account of the rarefied nature of what he is saying. He is writing as though all literature was like Mallarmé, existing entirely separately from the author, in an impersonal world of its own. Who is going to be impressed when you tell people that they have misread *Bleak House*, when they took it to be about Victorian England, and not about itself? Dickens is usually read for his referential value: as though he said something about the world he inhabited, rather than as though his text only commented on the language from which it emerged. Paul de Man seems to keep the concept of 'literature', but denies it the power to mean actively in the real world, in society. Since writers historically have changed society through their influence – Milton, Voltaire, Victor Hugo, Ruskin, Dickens himself, for example – it seems a poor argument that denies them or literature either that function, or, indeed, that possibility. And if texts do deconstruct themselves, it is hard to see why they should have been so continually misinterpreted, or taken in one way only.

It is worth comparing this viewpoint with Sartre's, in his influential *What is Literature?* of 1948, where the desire to use language to shape a future society is evident. He would have agreed that prose has the power to alter things: he sees it as having a very functional aim altogether, whereas he would say that poetry fails – at least in its present moment – to make contact with society, so that all that happens is that a poet such as Mallarmé virtually destroys the world in writing his poetry, where the words exist in their own materiality and hardness. In poetry, words signify, and thus reach beyond themselves. Sartre's Marxism makes him wish to put literature to political use; at the least he held that it gives to its readers an 'unhappy consciousness' of themselves: they learn more through it of their objective situation.

De Man's position is different, in that the normal distinction between prose and verse is not maintained, any more than it is in Paul Valéry, who identifies prose with utilitarian communication, and poetry with all poetic language. Paul de Man remains sceptical that literature could have practical use. He could well have replied to my objections that the uses to which literature have been put are neither here nor there: literary language knows itself to be mere repetition, fiction and allegory, and insofar as it is these things, if people have read it for its spontaneous message, they have performed their own closure on the work, as Derrida would have it: they have deliberately limited the play of its significance. How would you respond to that point?

DISCUSSION

1   The argument that a text can only be made to mean something by a willed act of interpretation is valid, surely, but it leaves out the point that has been implicit in my argument all along: that, historically, people have taken meanings from literature and have used those meanings to construct a strongly ideological sense of themselves and of the world. Leavis' near-reverential sense of the power of literature to affirm 'life' is only one example of this. To forget about meaning is to forget about history. Sartre would add the point that the quest for meaning is an obligation: in that sense, it hardly matters that all readings are misreadings, for the impulse towards meaning is linked to things that are outside the specific text: i.e. what meanings do we want to establish? Which is like asking, what sort of society do we want?

2 And if all literature is repetition, then do we need to add the adjective 'mere'? Paul de Man has also been interested in Maurice Blanchot, the French writer and critic, deeply influenced by Mallarmé and Nietzsche. He quotes Blanchot: 'We always write the same thing over again, but the development of what remains the same has infinite richness in its very repetition'. The repetition compulsion, in Freud's thinking, could involve lifting of a repressed memory, and thus prove valuable in its very unsettlingness; besides, the impulse to repeat for Blanchot, has to do with the feeling that because of that compulsion, there is growth of understanding. Blanchot, like de Man, was touched by the Hegelian tradition that insists that understanding is historical: to understand Shakespeare in the twentieth century is to take him very differently from the seventeenth- or nineteenth-century understandings; in the repetition of reading, something happens: greater self-consciousness develops. Blanchot defines literature as 'the question put to language by language become literature'.[3] That very Hegelian statement, which suggests that literature has the power to modify language at a very deep level, takes us way past the idea that literature tells us something, communicates simply. If it does communicate, that says much more about the way we have chosen to read the text, to enact our own enclosure upon it.

With these statements about literary language in mind, take this first stanza of a long poem by Hopkins, 'The Wreck of the Deutschland':

> Thou mastering me
> God! giver of breath and bread;
> World's strand, sway of the sea;
> Lord of living and dead;
> Thou hast bound bones and veins in me, fastened me flesh,
> And after it almost unmade, what with dread,
> Thy doing: and dost thou touch me afresh?
> Over again I feel thy finger and find thee.

These lines were written as the prelude to a poem concerning a shipwreck (in 1875) where five nuns, amongst many others, were drowned. In looking at it, you will certainly find it easy to isolate features of its structure: assonance, alliteration, strong rhythm, use of enjambement, caesura, and you should have a sense of the shifts of tone within it. You will see how words run into each other: breath /bread; bound/bones; dead/dread; finger/find, for example, and you will note the ambiguities of sense: 'sway of the sea' suggests God's rule over the tides (his sway) as well as the movement of the tides themselves — their swaying to and fro? In these ways, which you should spend time looking at, as an exercise, you will see how the 'literariness' of the passage advertises itself.

But after you have done this, ask yourself whether you feel that Paul de Man's statements apply to it. What kind of rhetoric is here? Are the lines self-reflexive? Do they belong to the public world at all, as indeed, they were originally intended to belong?

DISCUSSION

My response would be that de Man has a point in arguing for self-reflexivity. Though the lines are directed at God ('Thou'), it is clear that the poem is a complex piece of rhetoric designed to persuade the writer, and the reader (who is always, it is worth mentioning, assumed to be the complete reader, the person who knows everything: God, in fact). The complexity of the lines seem to me the proof of it. Its difficulty is rooted in the desire to ground the sentiments it expresses in some form of reality – and that reality can only be the poem itself. In the poem, if nowhere else, God is what Hopkins would like him to be: mastering, taking over, while the poem spills over into something like (but not quite) incoherence, kept tightly under control.

Hopkins would not, of course, have known anything of Saussure and the idea of the arbitrariness of the signifier. More, he would never have allowed, contrary to de Man, that what he writes is 'fiction'. Nonetheless, his poem could not be so dense, so full of 'literary language', I would argue, if he had not wanted to make the poem do what the shipwreck seemed to refuse – that is, to reaffirm reality in the midst of arbitrariness.

It seems to me that this is why 'practical criticism' remains important, so long as it does not simply confirm the critical position of the person doing it. The effort to discover how and where significance resides in the text is a 'performative' one, to use again J. L. Austin's term: it is actually utopist. That is, criticism tries to create significance. A text performs a work on the reader. When Billie Holliday sings 'These foolish things remind me of you', she refers to the trivia of the phone ringing, and a forgotten airline ticket, and so on, in their power to evoke nostalgic memories of a past lover. Actually, far more nostalgia is generated by the song, its tune and performance, than by any of the foolish things remembered, which are, of course, fictional: the song thus becomes performative, constitutive of reality for all those who hear, dance to, or hum along with the lyric. And that constitutive role is further – if not exclusively, in the case of the poetic text – brought out by 'practical criticism', with its emphasis on what the text does. Perhaps critics put it the wrong

way round, saying that 'the text says this . . .' whereas what is meant
is 'the text can be read in this way, and this perspective adopted on it
makes it a text reaching towards a possibility which it tries to turn
into reality'. The 'reality' is within the text itself, as the artefact taken
in a sense as full as possible. Criticism may fasten on the literariness
of language in order to find a defiance of the idea of arbitrariness: an
assertion through form, through the poetic function, of something to
move towards.

Heidegger might be mentioned in this connection. His readings
of German poets such as Hölderlin and Rilke have drawn attention
to poetic language as that which most importantly rivals philosophical thought, in that ordinary philosophical thinking works
representationally: that is, it names the world in terms that reduce
each entity in it to objects. But poetry does not reduce the world to
such categories: it names what other types of language overlook by
this procedure, or are incapable of expressing. Philosophical thought
cannot bear ambiguity, the play of many meanings: Heidegger insists
that 'the element in which thinking must move itself in order to be
rigorous is ambiguity'.[4] The 'thinking' here is poetic, not philosophical: while Heidegger maintains that 'language itself is poetry in the
essential sense',[5] he sees ordinary uses of language deviating from
this original poetry, which is itself crucial, since it 'first brings beings
to word and to appearance' (p. 73). Heidegger would wish for a
literature giving a structure of total complexity. Language uses
customarily conceal reality ('Being', as Heidegger calls it): in poetic
language, Being is brought into presence, starts up into consciousness. Literary language becomes, indeed, performative. It is worth
contrasting Heidegger's emphasis with J. L. Austin's in *How to Do
Things with Words*, where language in poetry is said to be 'in ways
parasitic upon its normal use'.[6] Heidegger takes normal language
uses (with grammar and syntax) to be an occlusion of the real,
following Nietzsche: both feel that poetic language draws previously
non-existent awarenesses and concepts into being.

An Example of Literature Beyond Understanding: Finnegans Wake

For Blanchot, reading is 'before or beyond the act of understanding'.
We might grasp that idea more easily in the light of the last chapter
and Kristeva's opposition to the symbolic order – to grammar, clear
sense, and to socially definable meaning. The text that most subverts
understanding in the obvious sense is surely *Finnegans Wake* (1939),
which deals with writing: 'the world, mind, is, was and will be
writing its own wrunes for ever', (p. 19). 'Wrunes' is a portmanteau
word suggesting both 'wrongs' and 'runes'. The 'world' spends its

time trying to correct its mistakes, and writing about the wrongs
done to it, and keeps on writing out hieroglyphics which it hopes will
last. That might be a description of 'intertextuality': there are no
'contexts' and standing out from them, special 'texts', but, rather, all
activity in the world is 'writing wrunes'; all the time using scraps of
past writing, past texts, which cannot change.

  Finnegans Wake deforms and questions language as it is organized into social use, and in that sense it goes as far as possible in
creating something that can reflect back, from its own autonomy, on
the intertexts that make up ordinary language. Here is the ending of
the end of the first part, the famous 'Anna Livia Plurabelle' section,
where the washerwomen on the banks of the Liffey discuss the
mother of the novel (who is also the river), and turn into elm and
stone as they talk and as the night falls. After you read it, think back
to the earlier Joyce passage quoted (from *A Portrait . . .*), and
consider how Joyce has moved on: think how different this is, too,
from Lewis Grassic Gibbon. But there are also rhythmic similarities,
as well as the deliberate creation of a language:

> Can't hear with the waters of. The chittering waters of. Flittering bats,
> fieldmice bawk talk. Ho! Are you not gone ahome? What Thom
> Malone? Can't hear with bawk of bats, all thim liffeying waters of.
> Ho, talk save us! My foos won't moos. I feel as old as yonder elm. A
> tale told of Shaun or Shem? All Livia's daughtersons. Dark hawks
> hear us. Night! Night! My ho head halls. I feel as heavy as yonder
> stone. Tell me of John or Shaun? Who were Shem and Shaun the living
> sons or daughters of? Night now! Tell me, tell me, tell me, elm! Night
> night! Telmetale of stem or stone. Beside the rivering waters of,
> hitherandthithering waters of. Night!   (pp. 215–6)

DISCUSSION

The obvious difference is that this text must be virtually created by
the reader, out of several languages (remember Derrida's commitment to this), there is, for instance, German, in 'halls' (echoes). You
cannot read this straightforwardly: it breaks with sense all the time,
and though Joyce read this passage out loud, on record, the whole
point of the excess of the signifier over the signified here is that so
many of the puns and the references are only intelligible by looking at
the spelling, not the pronunciation. You cannot, that is, read it in a
unitary way.

  Read aloud, the listener gets one text, read silently, the reader
gets another. I think it important that Joyce did read this passage out;
for it draws attention to language as something aural: when much
poetry was written to be sung, as in Elizabethan times, the point

would have been taken better. It may be argued that Saussure's attention to the arbitrariness of the signifier–signified relationship, playing down such concepts as onomatopoeia, deceives. We are so used to silent reading and on the whole unenthusiastic about public readings of poetry, that one half of what comprises 'literary language' goes missing: the aural. The Bob Dylan song quoted points the way towards a poetry that *does* use the heard quality of language. (Ezra Pound was not being perverse when, in an essay entitled 'Vers Libre and Arnold Dolmetsch', he defined poetry as 'a composition of words set to music': historically, that was true of earlier lyric forms.) Jakobson sees poetic language increase 'the palpability of the sign', and here language receives a 'double articulation' from its dual existence: as sound, and as sense. It is no coincidence that Jakobson quoted Valéry favourably: 'the poem is a prolonged hesitation between sound and meaning'.[7] Not only is there a double take – the text is both aural and visual – but the sense of the sound ties the poem back to referentiality, makes the text more, not less, in touch with the body, with the external world.

Here, then, in *Finnegans Wake* a text goes in two directions at once. Aurally, it works, in Joyce's reading, to evoke reality in a way that denies the idea of the arbitrariness of the signifier. In sense-terms, reality is under change. That fits the situation, which is one of metamorphosis. Night is falling, and distinctions are lost: the washerwomen lose their identity as they are metamorphosed, and perhaps their gender too, if they become 'stem or stone' – tools used for cleaning laundry, as well as elm and stone. As they go into night, so the image of the flow of water (undifferentiated: though there are some five thousand river names in this chapter: you may notice some in this section), is more and more appropriate: water, too, lacks identity, hardness of edge, as night does. The sense of transgression or regression is strong in the desire for gossip (dirty linen?), in the suggestions of incest ('daughtersons'), and in the need to hear, like children, a bedtime story. All stories seem to merge into one: they may repeat the sense of a primal sexual transgression, and the repeated impulse to hear (note how repetition structures the passage) tries to lift the repression that prevents the articulation of that primal knowledge (to do with the discovery of infantile sexuality), or that codifies it into socially acceptable forms.

Whose Interests does Literary Language Serve?

The break-up of standard ways of thinking and writing, performed here by Joyce, is the radical activity asked for in Julia Kristeva.[8] It illustrates a central argument of feminist theory enshrined in writers

such as Kristeva herself, Hélène Cixous, Luce Irigaray and Monique
Wittig, which states as a strong objection to many assumptions in the
discussion of 'literary language' that you cannot simply speak about
a generalized, and non-gendered language in literature: the question
first must be asked, *whose* language?

The argument is first urged by Virginia Woolf in *A Room of
One's Own* (1929) that the bulk of literature that has been written,
historically, is men's writing: so that epics and plays, and most
novels, represent the achievements of male ways of thinking. In her
last chapter she suggests that male writing is marked out by the
presence of the male ego, the 'I' that constantly asserts itself. Hence,
feminist readings would justly point to the fittingness that, in a body
of poetry usually addressed to the woman, and aiming to make love
to her, John Donne should refer to 'my words' masculine persuasive
force' (Elegy XVI, 'On his Mistress'). The assumption that persuasiveness is a male attribute goes with the construction of male
behaviour in culture: as something assertive, and demanding its way
with women. Woolf's response to that proposition about male
modes of writing is double: mainly she suggests that people should
reach to an androgynous position in life and writing where they do
not think in specifically male or female ways: but sometimes she
anticipates a position that has been adopted by some forms of French
feminism, and which proposes, following Lacan and Derrida, that
the entry into language is itself deforming, since it is the access to an
order that privileges, in its very warp and woof, the male. It is not
only 'logocentric', Derrida's term for a thinking that makes the
signifier the bearer of single meaning, but 'phallogocentric'.

Following Freud's *Three Essays on Sexuality* (1905), where the
bisexuality of infants – their 'polymorphous perversity' is touched
on, and made the foundation for all later sexual behaviour, it is
argued that the entry into language – into the symbolic order – is
repressive, constructing the gender of the child, and making him/her
identify for ever with one or other sex – with fundamental loss
resulting. Repression is the clue: the forms that language takes –
metaphor and metonymy, condensation and displacement – are
brought about from it; the repressed returns in moments when the
symbolic order is overthrown, as in jokes, dreams, Freudian slips.
These arguments will be familiar from Chapter 4. The washerwomen's talk in *Finnegans Wake* seems to go over stories that by
their repetitive effect, try to get at the repression covering over
children's early sexuality, a repression that operates fundamentally
in the stabilising effects of ordinary language.

If conventional language, implying gender types, people's place
in class, race and what expectations they can have, exists as

repression, it will also follow the conventions of dominant groups in the way it operates. 'Literary language' is not just, in its most developed and accepted sense, a *male* literary language, it is also, as used currently in Western educational circles *white*, and *middle class*. Kristeva's work, her *sémanalyse*, involves a critique of meaning, of its elements and its laws. In contrast, she looks for a literature that will develop the semiotic consciousness. We return to the stress on the aural, as a way of suggesting that language may be embedded within somatic, unconscious drives. (Children in language acquisition learn to dissociate the sound from the sense of a word. To bring back the stress on the aural, which is a real possibility with literary language, invites a different mode of attending: an unlearning of the conventions that exist in the world that stress only clear-cut sense. French feminism has suggested that patriarchal culture itself stresses looking to the detriment of hearing: and that this downplaying of the aural sense involves a cutting out of the feminine. Its restoration becomes then wholly important. But discussion of poetry, for instance, is more usually confined to the sense rather than the sound: the point holds strongly with the Anglo-American tradition.) Kristeva links the semiotic order, discussed in Chapter 6 with the maternal and feminine, and has looked for signs of it in such male writers as Lautréamont, Mallarmé and Céline.

One central inspiration has been Joyce's work, for here conventional – and repressed – meaning is overthrown. Perhaps something of the semiotic consciousness is regained in its rhythmic playfulness, and ability to hold plural possibilities. At one point, the book is described as 'this allnights newseryreel' (p. 489), and it is easy to see what implications exist in that. The idea of 'night' breaks up the clear order of day, where everything is seen in order and clarity, and gives the suggestion of the dream, where the symbolic order is certainly suspended. Then 'newseryreel' implies 'nursery-rhyme' – which would include the stories told to children – all of which, of course, by their insertion of children into narrative structures, enact a repression upon their fantasies, and 'newsreel' which flashes up images to be watched in the dark: here it is relevant, perhaps, that such writers as Christian Metz on cinema suggest that the enjoyment of the screen is a regressive one: a desire to return to the 'Imaginary' state, to the condition before repression. Joyce's language is thus interested in getting back to an understanding that precedes the ordered one of the public order of language. And no doubt there are many other associations, even in this quotation: the point is that *signifiance* is generated through the quotation, as through the whole book.

Similarly, Hélène Cixous, in a punning language with Joycean affiliations, writes to celebrate the feminine body: her essay 'The laugh of the Medusa' bids the writer 'beware of the signifier that would lead you back to the authority of a signified'. A text that evokes plurality, that refuses single meanings, that foregrounds the body and not intellectual concepts is sought after: the only French texts that Cixous sees as being feminine are by Colette, Marguerite Duras and Jean Genet. Luce Irigaray, in her *Ce sexe qui n'en est pas un*, puns on 'un' to mean 'not a male sex' (and therefore, in general estimation, hardly a sex at all), and 'not a single sex' – that is, not one marked by unitary thinking, by the demand for meaning, by the insistence on the priority of a single signified. To attend to Irigaray and Cixous would suggest that a literary language that opposes the primacy of the signified over the signifier, and that allows for the possibility of difference, that breaks up hard distinctions that have been culturally formed, is characteristically, in its opposition to male 'phallogocentrism', feminine.

These are points not at all addressed by critics in the Anglo-American traditions discussed in the second chapter. In their insistence on language being used in an exploratory, heuristic way, in all the setting aside of pre-determined meaning, there is never the sense that poetic language should not reach the public world and the common reader. There is a fundamental divide here. Leavis, in an article in *Scrutiny* (1933) called 'James Joyce and the revolution of the word' (a title re-used by Colin MacCabe in 1979, in an influential book setting out a totally contrary position, based closely on post-structuralism, especially in Barthes, as I discussed him in Chapter 2) saw *Finnegans Wake* as a decreative use of language: private, uninformed by a communal set of values, not allowing for new possibilities, but a cul-de-sac.

But then, the arguments of contemporary French feminism, the sense that language uses are heavily ideological, the belief that a text reflects the ideology of the *langue* it springs from, and above all, the politicizing of the issues of literature – these are all foreign to the critics with the views expressed in Chapter 2. Thus the sense that poetic uses of language break into new possibilities of meaning, which has been a base-note of so many theorists mentioned or discussed, is going to mean radically different things. Whether there is a common meeting point at all here I leave as a question.

With these opposing positions in mind, take as a final example of literary language, this description from Virginia Woolf's *Mrs Dalloway* (1925), a text looked at earlier for its use of the metaphoric axis of language to attempt to disrupt the commonsensical, oppressively patriarchal, onward plodding progress of time and phallogo-centric culture. The extract here gives Mrs Dalloway's sense of being frozen into separateness, initially, she thinks, in relation to her husband. I will leave you to think how this passage is also a reflection on the author's desire to write in such a way that cold, hard units of meaning will be broken down, and *significance* restored. This also entails the replacement of the symbolic order with something warmer, more immediate altogether, perhaps Kristeva's semiotic condition. Look at the rhythms (recall the letter from Woolf quoted in Chapter 5), the imagery, the use of repetition, the break-up of hard distinctions of time and of the sexes; and the way the passage both has links going right across it, uniting it as a meditation, but also opens itself up for enlarged significance, beyond the immediate situation:

> ... suddenly there came a moment – for example on the river beneath the woods at Cliveden – when, through some contraction of this cold spirit, she had failed him. And then at Constantinople, and again and again. She could see what she lacked. It was not beauty; it was not mind. It was something central which permeated; something warm which broke up surfaces and rippled the cold contact of man and woman, or of women together. For *that* she could dimly perceive. She resented it, as a scruple picked up Heaven knows where, or, as she felt, sent by Nature (who is invariably wise); yet she could not resist, sometimes yielding to the charms of a woman, not a girl, of a woman confessing, as to her they often did, some scrape, some folly.
>
> (Granada edition, 1976, pp. 29–30)

DISCUSSION

Some points that you might like to pursue further:

1   In the light of this chapter, would you want to think of 'literary language' as being something utopian, something aspired towards as a radical ideal? So that the literary becomes a way of writing that challenges meaning, (conventional, patriarchal, and currently bourgeois) as part of the fixed, symbolic system? If so, is this just a twentieth-century conception?

2   How useful is it, do you think, to stay with the concept of literary language? Does it make sense to go on using the idea of the literary? Or does it fix a 'canon' of literature too much and too partially to be helpful?

3   How would you want to arbitrate between the opposing positions outlined – that language in the symbolic order represses meaning and *significance*, or that its creative use focuses meaning and significance completely? Does Woolf help here? Is the split a basic division of opinion?

4   In the course of this text, I have tried to give as many definitions of literature, of poetry, prose, of the literary, as I can. All of them are ideological positions, of course, but some will have stronger claims than others. Which ones seem to you most useful now?

Appendix: Critical, Rhetorical and Technical Terms

Amplification of some of the terms used throughout the book, and suggestions of how to examine a text are given here; I hope they may be of practical value. I also look at the question of rhetorical tropes in literature, and ask what kind of value this enumeration of conventions within speech-uses has: this is an open question for the reader to ponder.

Formal Conventions

The technical terms used here are all familiar in traditional discussions of literary language, though the criticism that emphasizes direct response has always played down the more technical features of verse, as a kind of suspect mathematics.

In approaching questions of examining the structure of a text, in verse or prose, **assonance** and **alliteration** should be familiar. The first refers to the correspondence of vowel sounds in different words: it makes a form of internal rhyme:

> We hissed along the polished ice . . .

(from Wordsworth's *Prelude*, Bk I. line 434, discussing ice-skating). Alliteration gives the recurrence of the same letter or sound in close succession:

> After life's fitful fever
> (*Macbeth* III. ii. 23)

In verse, the effect of **enjambement** and the **caesura** should be noted. Enjambement is finely illustrated in Donne – 'I wonder by my troth, what thou and I / Did, till we loved?' ('The Good-Morrow') – it is the run-on from one line to the next, so that there is a strong emphasis on 'Did'. The effect amounts to: 'What on earth could we have been doing?' Much verse depends on the run-on: where the sense ends with the end of a line, the verse is called **end-stopped**.

A caesura is a break in the midst of a line. E.g.

> The waves beside them danced, but they
> Outdid the sparkling waves in glee
> ('The Daffodils' – Wordsworth)

Here the caesura is after 'danced'. Note that the caesura requires a new emphasis contrasting the waves and the daffodils – 'they'. You might also notice the enjambement which makes 'outdid' so emphatic. Is it to do with the way the mouth has to open as in a kind of gasp for breath to take in the initial vowel, the 'o'?

In reading verse, **rhythm, pace** and **tone** are important. Changes of tone especially, are crucial: in what *tone* of voice is this to be read? *Rhythm* is something that attaches itself to every utterance, even to 'Go and put the kettle on', and to work out the appropriate rhythm and pace is argued by Leavis to be a matter of learning to read sensitively. Titles of books are crucial for rhythmic qualities. Look at these titles:

> *Murder in the Cathedral*
> *Murder on the Nile*
> *Murder on the Orient Express.*

Note how the third seems to have within it the rhythm of the train; this is not **onomatopoeia**, which is where the sound of the word(s) describes/imitates the action, but it is quite like it in mimetic quality. The second title sounds less energetic – perhaps because of the long 'i' in 'Nile': appropriate for a stately cruise down the river. The first title juxtaposes two opposite ideas – murder and cathedral – for shock value.

In poetic language, **diction** and **syntax** are relevant considerations. The first has to do with the style or vocabulary adopted by the writer. Is it elevated, dignified, heroic, ordinary, colloquial or downright coarse? Again, shifts of diction within the same text will be important. The diction is not always apparent without detailed background knowledge. The Green Knight, in the anonymous medieval English poem *Sir Gawain and the Green Knight*, rides into

Arthur's hall, and demands 'Where is the governor of this gyng?'
Does 'gyng' just mean 'gang', and if so, is the diction of the Green
Knight rude and contemptuous? Or is he, as some Medievalists
suggest, being courteous? Is 'gyng' just a synonym for 'company'? A
dictionary is likely to prove of limited value here, and any assessment
requires a consideration of the cultural context: though the question
rises as to the relation between the text and the context: does the text
work alongside the period and the age, or does it quarrel, take issue
with it? Syntax involves the word-order, the sentence construction.
In poetry, this frequently draws attention to itself as odd or distinctive, deviating from the norm. The apparently direct syntax of the
Donne we have quoted compares oddly with Milton's opening:

> Of Man's first disobedience, and the fruit
> Of that forbidden tree, whose mortal taste
> Brought death into the world, and all our woe
> With loss of Eden, till one greater Man
> Restore us, and regain the blissful seat,
> Sing, heavenly Muse . . .
>   (*Paradise Lost* Book 1)

The syntax is Latinate, which involves it placing the main verb near
the end – 'Sing'; note here how much emphasis it receives by its
placing. The style is noble, heroic, non-colloquial. Note the repeated
caesurae and enjambements, the compressions – 'mortal taste',
which means 'taste by mortals' and 'taste which was deathly'. In
passing, pick out the early alliterations, and the assonance on 'us'
and 'bli*ss*ful'. Note, too, how this invocation to the Muse – a start
traditional to the classical epic – actually prevents a clear sense of
sequence of time emerging. (Though he begins with the word 'first' –
he will actually start the action of the poem *in medias res* – in the
middle of things, as Horace (*The Art of Poetry*) said all epics should
start, so there is, effectively, no 'first' disobedience at all.) The tenses
shift, which is part of the evasiveness this syntax permits. When does
the greater man restore us? William Empson would say there was an
ambiguity there. Was it, or will it be Christ? Will it be some successor
to Cromwell, as Christopher Hill's readings of the poem would
imply? How would you scan the first line?

> Of Man's first disobedience, and the fruit

It could be taken with the stress on man, dis, bed, and, fruit, which
would give a straightforward *iambic* (see below), or it could be given
a first stress on 'first', which would make the 'Of man's' an *anapaest*
(again, see below). If the second scansion was allowed, would it

suggest that Milton was obsessed with the idea that disobedience is perpetual – and that it could be seen in his own lifetime, with the Restoration of the monarchy? Discussion of syntactical structure and scansion becomes inseparable from discussion of a possible range of meaning: it means something very different, and somehow something not quite straightforwardly logical, because it is not set out as a piece of prose. It would be something very different if it were set out in a prose paraphrase.

Verse forms are important. Milton uses the blank verse **iambic pentameter** of ten or eleven beats with five stresses; Renaissance handbooks of rhetoric categorized the different ways that the accent can fall.

1 With the **iambus**, there is an unstressed syllable followed by a

    ˘ / ˘ / ˘ / ˘ / ˘ /

stressed – 'The curfew tolls the knell of passing day'.

2 With the **trochee**, a stress is followed by a non-stress, as with the

    / ˘ / ˘˘

opening of *Daniel Deronda* – 'Was she beautiful?', where the third word illustrates the next category; the

3 **dactyl**, which is a stressed syllable followed by two unstressed

    / ˘ ˘

ones. 'Heavenly' in the Milton quotation provides another example.

4 The **anapaest** is the reverse: two unstressed syllables leading to a stressed one: not frequent in English in a single word. Tennyson's

    / ˘ ˘ /

'Tears, idle tears' is a trochee which turns into an anapaest.

5 The **spondee** gives two stressed syllables together. Consider the

    / /

force of the word 'Outdid' in 'The daffodils' here.

Verse ends either with a masculine (stressed) syllable, or an unstressed (feminine) one. (The sexism of the language here which makes the weak ending feminine is unfortunate.) Eliot's 'familiar compound ghost' passage in part 2 of *Little Gidding* plays on the alternation of these endings:

    ˘ / ˘ / ˘ / ˘ / ˘ / ˘
For last year's words belong to last year's language [feminine]
    ˘ / ˘ / ˘ / ˘ / ˘ /
And next year's words await another voice. [masculine]

Stanza lengths may be dealt with easily: quatrains and octaves (four and eight line blocks) are most standard; but the sonnet – which comprises 14 lines, octave and sestet (Petrarchan), three quatrains and couplet (Shakespearian, as in 'Th'expense of spirit) is also very common, and should always be recognized.

Iambic pentameter is most common; but there is also the **trimeter**, with three stresses per lines, the **tetrameter** (Wordsworth's 'The daffodils' – a very familiar metre: the 'de-dum-de-dum-de-dum-de-dum' variety), with four, the **hexameter** or **alexandrine** for six feet, (as with Wilfred Owen's 'Exposure'), and the **fourteener**, which has seven stresses. Free verse (vers libre) of course attacks these conventions, and works away from regular stresses – as in Lawrence, Eliot, and Ezra Pound, who said about his early career as a 'Modernist' poet in London, 'to break the pentameter, that was the first heave' (Canto 81).

Stress (or 'accent') is usually held to give the distinction between prose and verse. Rhythm, or flow, is based on 'accent', and according to R. F. Brewer, 'the measured undulation of accented and unaccented syllables . . . (is) . . . its essential feature, without which it becomes mere prose'. Even in free verse, T. S. Eliot argues that 'the ghost of simple metre should lurk behind the arras in even the freest verse, to advance menacingly as we doze, and withdraw as we rouse' ('Reflections on Vers Libre'). Distinctions between prose and verse have become problematic over the last two hundred years or so: Rousseau in his Notebooks wondered 'How to be a poet in prose', and both the nineteenth century prose-poem (such as that of Mallarmé) and free verse itself could be seen as special cases that superficially, at least, trouble people in their attempts to distinguish poetry and prose. Robert Lowell, the American poet, however (to give the other side of the argument), said, 'I no longer know the difference between prose and verse', and T. S. Eliot isolates the difference by saying that 'Verse, whatever else it may or may not be, is itself a system of *punctuation*; the usual marks of punctuation themselves are differently employed'.[1] This suggests that the line becomes a unit of sense in verse, so that poetry involves a double reading: of the sense of each line, and the grammatical sense which the punctuation may allow for. In this double sense, grammar and logic are, if not overthrown, at least tested: the poem becomes unparaphrasable.

Figures of Speech and Figures of Thought

The tropes called **metaphor** and **metonymy**, discussed in Chapter 4, are part of a whole system of rhetorical terms, categorized in the medieval handbooks of rhetoric, giving the *ars dictaminis* (the art of letter-writing: itself seen as a form of artistic prose, and important for official letters and documents). These handbooks devoted themselves to 'the art of speaking well in secular matters': an early definition of literary language.

Bede, (673–735), for example, in his *De schematibus et tropis* (Concerning figures and tropes) categorized a formidable number of rhetorical uses of language.[2] 'Figures' differ from 'tropes': the first term refers to arrangements of words designed to achieve special effects. The second term applies when radical changes have been made to words themselves to indicate a change or turn of thought. The distinction is interesting, affecting as it does matters of tone, or of straightforward questions of style: irony, for instance, is often conveyed through figures of speech. Figures of thought have less to do with outward style, and deal rather with the way that thought keeps becoming double, non-unitary in sentences, and in Derrida's terms, characterized by *différance*. Obvious figures of thought are simile, metaphor and allegory. A **simile** is straightforward:

> I saw Eternity the other night
> Like a great Ring of pure and endless light . . .
> Henry Vaughan (1621–1695): 'The World'

The comparison of Eternity to the ring (a standard symbol of infinity) is turned, by the end of the same poem, into a metaphor, where the poet describes hearing the 'madness' of people's speculations about Heaven:

> But as I did their madness so discuss
>   One whispered thus,
> This Ring the Bride-groom did for none provide
>   But for his Bride.

The 'ring' of the beginning has struck in size to become a wedding ring: Vaughan is playing with words, not concepts. The simile (image) of the ring at the beginning has turned into a metaphor – no comparison is being made; the ring exists in its own right – and it is associated with other metaphors – of Christ as the Bridegroom, and the soul as the Bride.

Allegory is sustained metaphor: in Dante's *Paradiso* (c. 1321), there are long stretches of the poem which, in describing Heaven, use the ring image literally, and work from there. Quintilian called a metaphor an 'abbreviated simile'. In Wordsworth, 'The waves . . . danced' is metaphor: the waves are being compared to people who are dancing. Fundamental to metaphor, usually, is the discovery of similarity in dissimilarity. (The point holds with Vaughan's poem.) Thus metaphor is associated with paradox, with extravagance, and 'conceitedness' – that is, with clever turns of wit. Fundamental to metaphor is that two things are articulated within it: concepts cease to be single, isolatable, and instead run together, so that the distinction between what is the subject and what the comparison disappears.

Bede's list gives seventeen figures of speech. I isolate only a few: **Prolepsis,** here, a term which ought to follow on later in time, as the result of an action, is placed earlier, anticipatively. Thus when Blake speaks of 'England's green and pleasant land', that is proleptic: England is not at present either green or pleasant, but it will be when we have built Jerusalem.

Zeugma is where one verb serves two different parts of a sentence, as in the seventeenth-century poet, Edmund Waller's song:

> Go lovely rose,
> Tell her that wastes her time and me . . .

Anadiplosis means repetition of words or phrases within a sentence for effect; there are other types of repetition, such as **anaphora,** where several lines of a poem start with the same word or phrase; or **epanalepsis,** as in the passage from *Paradise Lost* (I. 27–9) that follows soon after what has already been quoted:

> *Say first* – for heaven hides nothing from thy view,
> Nor the deep tract of hell – *say first* what cause
> Moved our grand Parents . . .

Repetition here belongs to a public, persuasive art. (Who is being persuaded? On the surface, it seems to be the Muse – actually, it is Milton telling himself what to do. The rhetoric gives his work a public status, which, in cold fact, considering Milton's actual position at the time of writing, he did not possess. Rhetoric here is **performative.**) Another form of repetition is **epizeuxis** (repetition of opening phrases – 'Comfort ye, comfort ye my people'). I do not believe that these terms exist in their original terminology as more than pedantry, but what is important is that rhetoric drew distinctions between different forms of repetition. Look at Dickens's reiterations of 'Fog' in the opening page of *Bleak House*. Here a public novelist, aware of his role as the preacher, uses the art of repetition, and if the terms help in making us aware of how designed and full of ploys the arts of speech are, they will also help in the deconstruction of the text's intentions.

Bede also singles out **paronomasia** (play on words which sound alike: punning). Derridean deconstruction has been deeply in-

terested in ways in which effects of meaning: such as puns, of course
may indicate the workings of the unconscious, which Lacan argued
has a linguistic basis. But interest in punning also belongs to earlier
periods, which also enjoyed the play of the signifier, not arguing for
the tying down of words to single, clear signification. Thus George
Herbert could write this, called 'Ana {Mary / Army} gram':

> How well her name an Army doth present
> In whom the Lord of Hosts did pitch his tent!

The sophisticated discovery of an anagram on 'Mary' turns into a
comment on Christ being born from Mary's womb. Here is a playful
'literary language', which also works to produce poems whose shape
imitates their meaning – as with Herbert's 'Easter Wings'.

Bede also gives alliteration and rhyme in the list, and finishes
with **polysyndeton** and **dialyton**. The first of these occurs when
conjunctions are repeated again and again (as Hemingway's *A
Farewell to Arms* deliberately repeats 'and' in the first paragraph, to
convey anonymity, boredom and flatness); the second reverses the
procedure and has clauses piled up against each other with no
connectives – as with the beginning of the extract from *Finnegans
Wake*.

For figures of thought, Bede cites such terms as **catachresis**, an
example of which would be 'Blind mouths!' (from Milton's *Lycidas*
– a term of contempt applied to the corrupt clergy of his day). A
catachresis is a deliberate abuse or misuse of words, and Foucault in
his *The Order of Things* pp. 110–15, sees it as fundamental to
language-use: all formulations are catachretic, since there can be no
'proper' use of words (e.g. no distinction between literal and figurative uses), as the relationship between the signifier and the signified is
always unfixed, not natural, or imposed by necessity. Thus catachresis, which attacks the sense that there is a logic to troping, stands
as a model for all tropes. Bede also gives such devices as the use of
antonomasia (where a womaniser is called 'a right Casanova'), or
epithet, (where a person gets a nick-name) or **synecdoche** (often
aligned with metonymy, though we have considered it alongside
metaphor); and word reversals, such as Milton putting 'Sing, heavenly Muse' at the very end of a sentence, as such figures. Further comes
hyperbole, euphemism, and **sarcasm**. These terms will, on the whole,
be more familiar than the figures of speech, and it needs emphasizing
that they each have to do with discovering (sometimes surprising)
connections between concepts and ideas, normally kept apart, and
accommodating these discoveries within a literary form.

Bede gives examples from the Bible of each of these rhetorical devices (aiming to show that artistic prose has good precedents for its use) and his list is certainly not exhaustive of the figures that rhetoricians found to give. If many of the distinctions seem arid, they nonetheless draw attention to the rhetorical basis, the artificiality of writing: an artificiality certainly consciously recognized by Roman and Medieval and Renaissance writers, who followed such ideas consciously. The more private, Romantic and nineteenth-century writers would not be held in by such rules, believing in inspiration over the following of literary practice – but even here, the reader may observe the unconscious falling into rhetorical habits (as well as the conscious use, for specific purposes, at times, as in Dickens, or Lawrence).

Deconstruction, especially 'Yale deconstruction' has stressed the importance of rhetorical devices in Romantic and post-Romantic poetry, in order to stress the artificiality of writing, rather than seeing it as something natural, charged with a plenitude of meaning.³ Critics who believe in a direct response to a poem or piece of prose, may leave the 'craft or sullen art' (Dylan Thomas) too much out of account in their belief in the writer's personal individual sincerity motivating the successful work and dictating its style. Philosophically, we may argue that rhetorical arts flourished in an historical moment where there was little or no stress on the individual author and on his/her personal subjectivity. Here, questions of individual sincerity were subdued to the arts of speech and writing. The historical moment that, speaking very generally, we may associate with Descartes and the birth of the concept of the unified subject, who is also the Author when it comes to literary texts, places less emphasis on rhetoric and more on personal style. The ebb and flow of attention paid to rhetoric – now again a subject to be studied – fits with the dominance or otherwise of the humanist concept of people as unified, centred subjects: that which the work of Nietzsche, Heidegger, Foucault and Derrida in literary terms (as well as Marx and Freud) has done so much to erode.

Lacan sees the 'figures of thought' capable of being held under the two master-terms of metaphor and metonymy. In that sense, rhetorical devices may show how the individual subject is structured by language that prevents single, unitary thought emerging: which arrests or defers the idea of clear, unambiguous meaning.

Notes

The place of publication of books cited is London, unless otherwise stated.

Chapter 1

1 The view that 'literature' gains a new meaning in the nineteenth century
   is strongly contested by René Wellek, in 'What is Literature?', in a
   compilation of that name, edited by Paul Hernadi (Bloomington:
   Indiana University Press, 1978). See also Alastair Fowler, *Kinds of
   Literature* (Oxford University Press, 1984).

Chapter 2

1 Matthew Arnold, 'The study of poetry', *Essays in Criticism* (Everyman
   edition, 1964), p. 237, for the discussion of the 'best poetry', (for the
   later quotation, where Arnold defends a 'real' i.e. value-laden, not
   'historic' estimate of poetry, see p. 240. I have also quoted from
   'Wordsworth', *op. cit.* p. 302, for the account of poetry as a criticism of
   life. I have also used the essay on Tolstoy, from where I have taken the
   quotation, that 'the crown of literature is poetry' (p. 353).
2 Shelley, opening of *A Defence of Poetry* (1821).
3 Walter Pater, 'The school of Giorgione', *The Renaissance* (1873; 1928
   edn. p. 128); Oscar Wilde, 'Preface' to *The Picture of Dorian Gray*, in
   Plays, Prose Writings and Poems (Everyman edition, 1930) p. 70.
4 F. R. Leavis, 'James as Critic', in *Henry James: Selected Literary
   Criticism* ed. Morris Shapira, (Heinemann, 1963) p. xvii; D. H.
   Lawrence, 'John Galsworthy', *Phoenix* (Heinemann, 1936) p. 539.
   Leavis quotes Hopkins on poetical language in *The Common Pursuit*,
   (1952, Harmondsworth 1962 p. 46). The same book supplies the
   Leavisian reference to a 'deep animating intention' within the text, (*op.
   cit.* p. 225); the phrase needs weighing for its similarities and differences
   to the New Critics' Intentionalist Fallacy. I have taken the references to
   Keats from the essay in *Revaluation* (1936, Harmondsworth 1964), and
   page references cited in the text are from that edition.
5 T. S. Eliot, *Selected Essays* (3rd edition, 1951) p. 145.
6 D. H. Lawrence, 'The Spirit of Place' in *Studies in Classic American
   Literature* (1924), quoted in Anthony Beal, *D. H. Lawrence: Selected
   Literary Criticism* (Heinemann, 1956) p. 297. The essay deals with

literature as 'art-speech', which is valued over ordinary speech in that, for Lawrence, it is 'the only truth'.

Chapter 3

1 Roland Barthes, *Writing Degree Zero* (New York: Hill and Wang, 1967) pp. 20, 67. Barthes, in an essay of 1960, published in *Critical Essays*, sees post-1850 literature making a distinction possible between the *écrivain* and the *écrivant*. (The distinction is from Sartre.) The first of these engages with writing: writing is an intransitive verb; has no object that is being worked on, while the second only works from meanings pre-given, uses language purely instrumentally, for information. The distinction is crucial for Modernist writing.

2 Stephan Mallarmé, 'Variations on a subject', *The Poems*, trans. Keith Bosley, (Harmondsworth, 1977) p. 49.

3 T. S. Eliot, *op. cit.* p. 289. The whole passage is relevant: 'The poet must become more and more comprehensive, more allusive, more indirect, in order to force, to dislocate if necessary, language into his meaning'. The essay belongs to 1921, the year before *The Waste Land*.

4 Jan Mukarovsky, 'Standard Language and Poetic Language' in *A Prague School Reader*, ed. Paul Garvin (Washington DC Georgetown 1964) p. 19.

5 Mikhail Bakhtin, *The Dialogic Imagination*, trans. Caryl Emerson and Michael Holquist, (Austin, Texas, 1981) p. 303.

6 Mallarmé, *op. cit.* p. 44–5. Bosley translates: 'The pure work implies the disappearance of the author as speaker, who hands over to the words, set in motion by the shock of their unevenness, they are lit by each other's reflections virtually like a train of flashes on precious stones . . .'. The disappearance of the author relates to important themes in Barthes, who wrote an essay called 'The death of the author' dealing with this theme (see *Image Music Text* (1977), to Michel Foucault ('What is an author?' – *Textual Strategies*, ed. J. Harari (Methuen, 1979)), and to Derrida's work, (see Chapter 6, below). In each case, what is at stake is the loss of the humanist concept of author as the privileged subject, the centre from whom meaning radiates out.

Chapter 4

1 Samuel Johnson, *Selected Writings*, edited Patrick Cruttwell (Harmondsworth, 1968) p. 476.

2 Stanley Fish, 'How Ordinary is Ordinary Language?', *New Literary History* 5 (1973) 41–54. (The whole issue is dedicated to the issue of literary language.) Fish's *Is there a Text in this Class?: the authority of interpretive communities* (Cambridge, Mass. Harvard University Press, 1980) sets out reception theory, and the way that texts are institutionally created as 'literary'.

3 Raymond Williams, *Marxism and Literature* (Oxford, 1977) p. 46. Williams' work on the history of the term 'literature' in *Keywords* (Fontana, 1976) pp. 150–4 gives an illuminating discussion of the uses of the word: he argues that the word 'poetry' covered the meaning of 'literature' as 'fine writing' before the rise of the novel necessitated the

use of the less specialized word, which also confined 'poetry' to metrical composition.

4 Jakobson's position, as described in this chapter, is most fully set out in his 'Closing statement: Linguistics and poetics', in T. A. Sebeok (ed.) *Style in Language* (Cambridge, Mass. Harvard University Press, 1960) pp. 350–77. The discussions of metaphor and metonymy are in Jakobson and M. Halle, *Fundamentals of Language* (Mouton: The Hague, 1956) part 2.

5 Anthony L. Johnson, 'Jakobsonian theory and literary semiotics', *New Literary History*, 1982, 33–61. It is not clear that Jakobson (as opposed to Saussure) plays down aural matters. On matters of aural patterning within poetic language, see the article by Derek Attridge, 'Language as Imitation: Jakobson, Joyce and the Art of Onomatopoeia', *Modern Language Notes* 1984, 1116–40. Attridge sees Jakobson's conception of the poetic bringing out the connection between the Saussure's signifier (the sound) and the signified (the concept): terms discussed further in Chapter 5. He quotes from Joseph Graham, 'Flip, Flap, Flop: Linguistics as Semiotics', *Diacritics* 11 (1981) 29–43, p. 33 – 'The poetic function, defined as a focus on the message for its own sake, renders meaning almost palpable by precipitating those features of language *especially appropriate for its representation*. Becoming the dominant function, it characterizes poetry as the most iconic or mimetic form of language' (my italics). In other words, the poetic use of language undermines the sense of the arbitrariness of the signifier, which is, of course, a leading point of structuralist analysis. ('Iconic' refers to C. S. Peirce's theory of semiotics, and describes signs which have some strong resemblance to their referent.)

6 *Shakespeare's Sonnets* edited by Stephen Booth, (Yale, New Haven, 1977). Jakobson's essay on Sonnet 129 appeared in collaboration with Lawrence Jones: *Shakespeare's Verbal Art in 'Th'Expence of Spirit'* (Mouton, The Hague, 1970).

7 Michael Riffaterre, *The semiotics of poetry* (Bloomington, Indiana University Press, 1978). Riffaterre's critique of Jakobson (and of Lévi-Strauss, Jakobson's colleague in New York after the war) is found in 'Describing Poetic Structures: two approaches to Baudelaire's "Les chats"', *Yale French Studies* 36/37, (1966) 200–42.

8 Julia Kristeva, *Desire in Language* (Oxford: Blackwell, 1980) p. 66.

Chapter 5

1 Ferdinand de Saussure, *Course in General Linguistics* (1915: Fontana, 1974) p. 120.

2 F. R. Leavis, *The Common Pursuit*, op. cit. p. 51.

3 Friedrich Nietzsche, *Twilight of the Idols* (1888, Harmondsworth, 1968 p. 38). Nietzsche's statement here should be supplemented in the light of his arguments in *The Genealogy of Morals* (1887) First Essay, XIII, which sets out the way that grammar imposes a grid upon experience.

4 Jacques Lacan, *Ecrits*, translated by Alan Sheridan (Tavistock Publications, 1977), pp. 146–78. This is certainly the essay to start with for Lacan. See p. 156 for the Victor Hugo illustration.

5 A further ambiguity suggests that Polly is singing solicitously that Macheath's life hangs by a thread: i.e. he (and therefore she) is in danger. But the ideology of the text referred to suggests the complete abandonment of all morality and its replacement by mere self-interest.

6 William Empson, *Seven Types of Ambiguity* (1930: Harmondsworth 1961) p. 205. I have given other page references in the text.

7 The edition of Owen edited by C. Day Lewis (Chatto and Windus, 1963), p. 49 gives 'His' in the text (following Edmund Blunden, Owen's first editor). The footnote, by Dennis Welland, reads: '*This* is a pencilled correction (above the line) of a previously inserted *the*. I am sure that it is *this*, but there is just enough ambiguity about it to justify retaining EB's preferable reading'.

8 Lacan, *op. cit.* p. 165. The anti-Cartesian statement of p. 166 is even more stark: 'I think where I am not, therefore I am where I do not think'.

9 On rhetoric there is a good introductory essay by Terry Eagleton, in *Walter Benjamin: towards a revolutionary criticism* (Verso, 1981). (This book, incidentally, contains an excellent discussion of Bakhtin.) There are many standard volumes on the topic, of which James J. Murphy, *Rhetoric in the Middle Ages* (University of California Press, 1974) is a good example. E. R. Curtius, *European Literature and the Latin Middle Ages* (Routledge and Kegan Paul, 1953) is a fundamental textbook for older understandings of literature, as in Erich Auerbach, whose *Literary Language and its Public* (Routledge and Kegan Paul, 1965) sets out a view of literary language in the period of the decline of the Roman Empire, as the language of the educated classes, characterized by selectivity, homogeneity and conservation – a view as far removed from modern senses as can be imagined.

10 Friedrich Nietzsche, *The Will to Power*, Section 481; see also Section 604. (ed. Walter Kaufmann, New York; Random House, 1967, p. 267, 327).

11 Quoted L. C. Knights, 'Restoration Comedy', *Explorations* (1946: Harmondsworth, 1964) p. 140. The essay by Knights 'Bacon and the seventeenth-century dissociation of sensibility' in this volume raises important issues about language uses that are relevant for this section on rhetoric.

Chapter 6

1 Plato, *Phaedrus*, trans. Walter Hamilton, (Harmondsworth, 1973) p. 101.

2 Jacques Derrida, *Disseminations* trans. Barbara Johnson (University of Chicago Press, 1981).

3 Jacques Derrida, *Memoires for Paul de Man* (New York: Columbia University Press, 1986) p. 15.

4 Derrida's work on Austin and Searle may be followed in the essays 'Signature Event Context', and in Searle's reply, 'Re-iterating the Differences: a Reply to Derrida', and Derrida's response, 'Limited Inc a b c', in *Glyph* 1 (Baltimore, Johns Hopkins Press, 1977).

5 T. S. Eliot, 'Poetry in the Eighteenth Century' (1930), reprinted in *From Dryden to Johnson* (Harmondsworth, 1963) p. 271.

6 Jacques Derrida, *Positions* (University of Chicago Press, 1981) p. 41.

The discussion of 'I have forgotten my umbrella' in *Spurs* (Chicago, 1978) pp. 123–43 takes its rise from the point that Nietzsche wrote the words in quotation marks. This already gives a quality of undecidability to the text: who is writing? Was he quoting? If so, it is interesting to speculate on the source, and the reason for wishing to retain the formulation. Can we interpret 'umbrella'? – psychoanalytically as the phallus: (but forgotten? Or folded up?) Is it a statement about Nietzsche's styles of writing (Derrida's subject in *Spurs*) – an umbrella can be used as a spur, stimulating, protecting, obtruding) – a matter of protecting the writer (the umbrella as pen-shaped – a pen is a 'stylo'; with folds which are veil/sail-like: (the French *voile* includes the ideas of sails and veils – covering and concealing); protecting the philosopher from single, univocal meaning (Nietzsche the deconstructionist), or from metaphysics? Or does the statement fit, metaphorically, with Heidegger's accusation that philosophers have forgotten the question of Being? Derrida, 'proving' that the text can mean all these things, shows how all deep interpretation (hermeneutics) is open to parody – though it might also be significant.

7 Julia Kristeva, *Revolution in poetic language* (New York: Columbia University Press, 1984) pp. 2–3. For a further account of 'signifiance', see Stephen Heath, *Roland Barthes: Image: Music: Text* (Fontana, 1977) p. 10. He quotes Barthes: '*signifiance* . . . is that radical work . . . through which the subject explores – entering, not observing – how the language works and undoes him or her'. In the work of signifiance, the self is lost, deconstructed – along with communicable meaning and thought. It thus connects with 'jouissance'.

8 T. S. Eliot, 'The Music of Poetry' (1942), *Selected Prose* ed. John Hayward, (Harmondsworth, 1953) p. 57; 'The Use of Poetry and the Use of Criticism' (1933), *op. cit.* p. 94.

9 D. W. Harding, *Experience into Words* (1963: Harmondsworth, 1974) p. 99. Harding's essay, originally published in *Scrutiny*, is commented on importantly by Leavis in *The Common Pursuit, op. cit.*, pp. 132–3: the essay is part of Leavis' definition of the tragic, and how this relates to the poetic use of language, with its capacity to generate 'signifiance'. *The Common Pursuit* also contains the essay 'Literature and Philosophy': Leavis' reply to Wellek.

Chapter 7

1 See *Textual Strategies* ed. Josué Harari (1980) p. 130. For further work on Paul de Man, see the compilation: *Rhetoric and form: deconstruction at Yale*, ed. Robert Con Davies and Ronald Schliefer, (Norman: University of Oklahoma Press, 1985).

2 Sartre, from whom de Man also derives, would have allowed for this questioning of the text to arise in poetry but not in prose, since poetry is self-referential, as prose is not. Prose has meaning (*sens*) but not *signification* (as poetry has) – this can only come from a signifying intention from outside. In *What is Literature?* (1948) the prose writer is defined as 'making use of words' for some other motive than just writing. (Compare Chapter 3, note 1.)

3 de Man's article on Blanchot is to be found in the useful *Modern French*

Criticism, ed. John K. Simon (University of Chicago Press, 1972). I have taken the second Blanchot quotation from Annette Lavers, *Roland Barthes: Structuralism and After* (Methuen, 1982) p. 64. The Simon anthology also has a fine article by Fredric Jameson on Sartre, and by Edward Said introducing structuralism.

4 Martin Heidegger, 'What calls for thinking', quoted in David A. White, *Heidegger and the Language of Poetry* (Lincoln: University of Nebraska Press 1978) p. 212. In this essay, Heidegger shows in what direction poetic language must go, when he examines a textual fragment of the Greek Parmenides, and begins by re-translating it from the conventional syntactic rendering 'One should both say and think that being is' into a paratactic (unconnected) formulation, 'Needful: the saying also thinking too: being: to be'. Heidegger stresses that the conventional syntactical translation establishes fixed relationships within the text, and this acts as an imprisonment of thought; whereas paratactic writing, breaking down conventional models, allows for a revealing of significance through the very absences, as well as presences, of the text. (This aspect of taking a text has been very influential upon Derrida, and his insistence that a text cannot be made to say a single statement.)

5 Martin Heidegger, 'The Origin of the Work of Art', *Poetry, Language, Thought* (New York, 1971) p. 74.

6 Contrast Heidegger's sense of priorities with J. L. Austin's, in *How to Do Things with Words* (1962) where language in poetry is said to be 'in ways *parasitic* upon its normal use' (quoted, White, *op. cit.*, p. 225 – Austin's emphasis.

7 The first quotation appears in Jakobson and Linda Waugh's *The Sound and Shape of Language* (Bloomington: University of Indiana Press, 1979) p. 231; the second is in *Style and Language*, edited T. A. Sebeok (MIT, Mass. 1960).

8 For Joyce's radicalism is the use of language, see Colin MacCabe, *James Joyce and the Revolution of the Word* (Macmillan, 1979) and the essays by Stephen Heath, in MacCabe (ed.) *James Joyce: New Perspectives* (Brighton: Harvester, 1982) and in Derek Attridge and Daniel Ferrer, *Post-structuralist Joyce* (Cambridge, 1984). For the feminism of Kristeva, Irigaray and Cixous, see the anthology by Elaine Marks and Isabelle de Courtivron, *New French Feminisms* (Brighton: Harvester, 1981), and Toril Moi, *Sexual, Textual Politics* (Methuen: 1985).

The question, 'whose language?' that feminists have posed, as a necessary prelude to dealing with issues of literary language, applies just as strongly to black groups, for instance, who have found it necessary (like Hugh MacDiarmid and Lewis Grassic Gibbon as far as Scottish literature is concerned) to oppose 'Standard English' as something bound up with questions of power and hegemonic control. Theoretical considerations of the national language as an ideology are taken up in Noelle Bisseret's *Education, Class Language and Ideology* (Routledge and Kegan Paul, 1979) (applied to France), and Linton Kwesi Johnson's poetry, for example, should certainly be looked at for its challenge to Standard English. Poems by Tony Harrison in the collection called 'The School of Eloquence' in *Selected Poems* (Harmondsworth, 1984) deal with the issue of 'Standard English' and 'Received Pronunciation', as they affect issues of literary language.

Appendix

1 Both statements are quoted by Christopher Ricks, in *William Wordsworth*, ed. Graham McMaster, (Harmondsworth, 1972) p. 505. Further help on prosody comes from G. S. Fraser, *Rhythm, Metre and Free Verse* (Methuen: 1970), and from Donald Wesling, *The New Poetries* (Lewisburg, Associated Universities Press, 1985).

2 For Bede's complete list, with examples, see the compilation by Joseph M. Miller, Michael H. Prosse and Thomas W. Benson, *Readings in Medieval Rhetoric* (Bloomington: University of Indiana Press, 1974). I have only dealt with examples which are still in use, judging from their listing in J. A. Cuddon, *A Dictionary of Literary Terms* (Andre Deutsch 1977). For further help on rhetoric, see above, Chapter 5 note 9. See also Roger Fowler, (ed.) *A Dictionary of Modern Critical Terms* (1973) and M. H. Abrams, *A Glossary of Literary Terms* (New York: Holt, Rinehart and Winston 4th edition, 1981), and Richard A. Lanham, *A Handlist of Rhetorical terms* (Berkeley: University of California Press, 1968).

3 For examples of approaches to literature on rhetorical lines, see Rosemond Tuve, *Elizabethan and Metaphysical Imagery* (University of Chicago Press, 1947), and Helen Vendler, *The Odes of John Keats* (Cambridge, Mass. Harvard University Press, 1983).

Further Reading

Few books have dealt with the topic of literary language, but see Winifred Nowottny, *The Language Poets Use* (Athlone Press, 1962) and Norman Page (ed.) *The Language of Literature* (Macmillan, 1984) for overviews on the subject in the light, mainly, of the arguments set out in Chapter 2.

For the material of Chapter 2, the reader should consult Leavis' practical criticism: in the magazine *Scrutiny* (1933–52); and his essays on the criticism of poetry in *The Living Principle* (Chatto and Windus, 1975) pp. 71–154, and 'How to Teach Reading' in *Education and the University* (Chatto and Windus, 1943). For other accounts of practical criticism, apart from I. A. Richards' book of that name (1929), see H. Coombes, *Literature and Criticism* (Hardmondsworth, 1953) and R. T. Jones, *Studying Poetry* (Arnold, 1986). Both of these give careful detail to 'the words on the page'.

For the issues in Chapter 3, see the various articles anthologized in Robert Young (ed.) *Untying the Text* (Routledge and Kegan Paul, 1981). On the changes associated with Flaubert's work, and its impact, see Jonathan Culler, *Flaubert: the Uses of Uncertainty* (Elek, 1974). Culler's work on Saussure, and Jakobson, in *Structuralist Poetics*, (Routledge and Kegan Paul, 1975), on Riffaterre and intertextuality in *The Pursuit of Signs* (R.K.P. 1981) and on Derrida and Yale deconstruction, (the theme of Chapter 6) in *On Deconstruction* (R.K.P. 1983) is all important, and was in its own time path-breaking for English readers.

A good starting article on Barthes may be found in John Sturrock's *Structuralism and After* (Oxford: Oxford University Press, 1979).

For Russian Formalism, see Lee T. Lemon and Marion J. Reiss, *Russian Formalist Criticism: Four Essays* (Lincoln: University of Nebraska Press, 1965). On the Prague circle, see J. Vachek, *A Prague School Reader* (Bloomington: University of Indiana Press, 1964). On Bakhtin, see Allon White in Frank Gloversmith (ed.) *The Theory of Reading* (Brighton: Harvester 1984).

For Chapter 4: on Jakobson, see Michael Lane (ed.) *Structuralism: a Reader* (Cape, 1970). For matters of stylistics, see Roger Fowler, (ed.) *Essays on Style and Language* (Routledge and Kegan Paul, 1966), and *Style and Structure in Literature* (Oxford, 1975). The anthologies by Seymour Chatman, *Literary Style: A Symposium* (Oxford, 1971) and *Approaches to Poetics* (New York: Columbia University Press, 1973) are important. Much work on stylistics seems improverished by not considering language as ideologically structured at any time: the *langue* of Saussure is Foucault's field of 'discourse', the existing state of ideological relations that allow certain things to be said in any historical conjuncture, and that prevent others. Thus, to contest dominant forms of discourse, as some literary language does, is to contest ideology. Foucault's work goes out of the sphere of this book, but his essays on literature and language are relevant: see *Language, Counter-Memory, Practice* (New York: Cornell University Press, 1977).

On metaphor (the most vast secondary literature of any literary topic exists on this subject), see Terence Hawkes, *Metaphor* (Methuen, 1972). *On Metaphor*, ed. Sheldon Sacks (University of Chicago Press, 1978) has important articles by Paul de Man and Paul Ricoeur. David Lodge gives excellent critical readings based on the metaphor–metonymy distinction in *The Modes of Modern Writing* (Arnold, 1977).

For Chapter 5, and Nietzsche on language, see the essays collected in David Allison, (ed.) *The New Nietzsche* (Cambridge: Mass. 1977). Vol. 14 of the Penguin Freud, 'Art and Literature' is full of implications for language use in literature. M. M. Mahood's *Shakespeare's Wordplay* (Methuen, 1957) is good on ambiguities in his texts. Lacan's work is difficult: a guide to the *Ecrits* may be found in John P. Muller and William J. Richardson *Lacan and Language* (New York: International University Press, 1982).

In Chapter 6, for Derrida, see Christopher Norris, *Deconstruction: Theory and Practice* (Methuen, 1982), and the same author's *William Empson and the Philosophy of Literary Criticism* (Methuen, 1978). Paul de Man's *Blindness and Insight* (New York and Oxford University Press, 1971) raises fundamental issues involved in Yale deconstruction. The secondary literature on Paul de Man is vast: see the note-reference to Chapter 7 note 1, and the bibliography in Harari; see also the journal *Diacritics* for its continual treatment of the issues central to the issues of Chapters 3 to 7 here.

Index of Names

Aristotle, 65, 68
Arnold, Matthew, 7, 10–15, 107
Attridge, Derek, 109
Auerbach, Erich, 110
Austen, Jane, 45–7
Austin, John L., 56, 74, 90, 91, 112

Bakhtin, Mikhail, 1, 27, 31–5, 52, 60, 73, 78
Barthes, Roland, 22–3, 26, 73, 76, 82, 84, 96, 108, 111
Beardsley, Monroe, 18, 87
Bede, 103–6
Blake, William, 104
Blanchot, Maurice, 88, 91
Brooks, Cleanth, 17, 18, 19

Cicero, 65, 66, 67
Cixous, Hélène, 94, 95
Coleridge, Samuel Taylor, 11, 12, 18
Culler, Jonathan, 73, 114

Dante, Alighieri, 67, 103
De Man, Paul, 18, 73, 86–91
Derrida, Jacques, 9, 18, 35, 71–6, 83, 88, 92, 94, 110, 111, 112
Dickens, Charles, 32–5, 38, 87, 104
Donne, John, 14–15, 17, 94
Dryden, John, 11, 44, 67
Duck, Stephen, 3–9, 12, 21, 39
Dylan, Bob, 82, 93

Eliot, George, 3–9, 14

Eliot, Thomas Stearns, 17, 23, 28, 35, 38, 66, 75, 79, 80, 101, 102, 108
Empson, William, 17, 19, 21, 54, 61, 80–1, 100

Fish, Stanley, 39, 40, 73, 108
Flaubert, Gustave, 23
Fleming, Ian, 6
Foucault, Michel, 1, 105, 114
Freud, Sigmund, 57–63, 73, 76, 89, 94
Frost, Robert, 22

Gay, John, 60–1
Gibbon, Lewis Grassic (James Mitchell), 81–2, 92

Harding Denys, W., 80
Heidegger, Martin, 83, 91, 112
Herbert, George, 63–5, 75, 105
Hobbes, Thomas, 3–9, 67
Holliday, Billie, 90
Hopkins, Gerard Manley, 13, 16, 17, 22, 44, 55, 61, 89
Hugo, Victor, 58–9, 87

Irigaray, Luce, 96

Jakobson, Roman, 8, 27, 29, 31, 36–54, 57–60, 93, 109
James, Henry, 12–15, 18, 19
Johnson, Samuel, 11, 12, 20, 36, 37, 75
Joyce, James, 35, 39, 69–71, 74, 85, 91–3, 95

Keats, John, 10, 15–17, 61, 65
Kristeva, Julia, 52, 78–91, 93

Lacan, Jacques, 58–63, 66, 76, 77, 78, 94, 106, 110
Lawrence, David Herbert, 12, 13, 19, 36, 69–71, 73, 107–8
Leavis, Frank Raymond, 1, 13–17, 19, 31, 35, 36, 40, 55, 73, 80, 88, 96, 107, 111
Lowell, Robert, 102
Lukács, Georg, 22, 26

Mallarmé, Stéphane, 23, 36, 51, 77–9, 88, 95, 102, 108
Marinetti, Filippo, 26
Marx, Karl, 3–9
Mayakovsky, Vladimir, 26, 29
Mill, John Stuart, 68
Miller, J. Hillis, 18, 87
Milton, John, 14, 15, 67, 87, 100–1, 104, 105
Mukarovsky, Jan, 28
Mulhern, Francis, 15

Nietzsche, Friedrich, 26, 55–7, 66, 68, 76, 91, 109

Olson, Charles, 68
Owen, Wilfrid, 16, 61–2, 102, 110

Pater, Walter, 13, 23
Plato, 65, 68, 71
Pope, Alexander, 3, 11, 67
Pound, Ezra, 2, 35, 68, 93, 102
Propp, Vladimir, 27, 30, 31, 35
Puttenham, George, 67

Quintilian, 65–7, 103

Ramus, Peter, 53
Ransom, John Crowe, 17
Richards, Ivan A., 17, 18
Riffaterre, Michael, 50–3, 77

Sartre, Jean-Paul, 88, 111
Saussure, Ferdinand de, 29, 30, 31, 40, 44, 54–7, 60, 90
Searle, John, 74
Shakespeare, William, 42–3, 49–53, 59, 62, 98, 102
Shelley, Percy Bysshe, 12
Shklovsky, Victor, 27–8
Sidney, Philip, 64, 85
Spenser, Edmund, 15–17
Sprat, Thomas, 67–8
Sterne, Laurence, 28–9
Stevens, Wallace, 23–5

Tolstoy, Leo, 27, 28, 63

Valéry, Paul, 84, 88
Vaughan, Henry, 103

Waller, Edmund, 104
Wellek, René, 17, 107
Wilde, Oscar, 13, 23
Williams, Raymond, 40, 108
Wittgenstein, Ludwig, 25
Woolf, Virginia, 47–8, 79, 94, 95–6
Wordsworth, William, 2, 12, 14, 17, 19, 68, 98, 99, 103